YOUNG STUDENTS
Learning Library

VOLUME 2

Amoeba–Astronomy

WEEKLY READER BOOKS
MIDDLETOWN · CONNECTICUT

PHOTO CREDITS

Young Students Learning Library is a trademark of Field Publications.

Copyright © 1990, 1989, 1988, 1982, 1977 Field Publications; 1974, 1972 by Funk & Wagnalls, Inc., & Field Publications.

ISBN 0-8374-6032-8

CONTENTS

AMOEBA Every time you drink a glass of water you swallow a number of amoebas. These creatures are made up of only a single cell—unlike ourselves; each of us contains many millions of cells. Amoebas are found in both fresh and salt water and in the soil. They also live inside human beings and animals. Most types are harmless, but one variety can cause a disease called amoebic dysentery in human beings. The common amoeba, called *Amoeba proteus* by scientists, is only 1/50 inch (0.5 mm) long.

An amoeba moves from place to place by pushing out part of itself. The pushed-out part is called a *pseudopod*. The amoeba pours the rest of its body fluids into the pseudopod—this is how it drags itself along. It also uses pseudopods to swallow tiny bits of food.

Amoebas reproduce by splitting. The nucleus of the original amoeba divides into two parts. Then the amoeba itself splits, forming two new amoebas, each with its own nucleus.

ALSO READ: CELL.

AMPERE, ANDRE MARIE (1775–1836) André Ampère was a French mathematician and scientist who studied electricity and magnetism. He was born at Polemieux, near Lyons, France. His father was beheaded during the violence of the French Revolution when André was 18. A few years later, André's wife died of tuberculosis. He was greatly depressed by the loss of his wife and father and tried to forget his sadness by working harder on his scientific experiments.

In 1820, Hans Christian Oersted, a Danish scientist, discovered that an electric current can move the needle of a compass. Ampère heard about the discovery, and seven days later, he was able to explain it by the use of mathematics. He also showed that

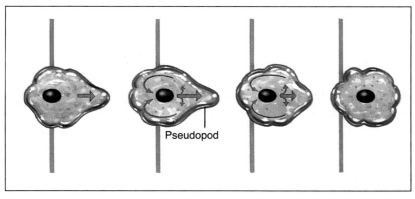

Pseudopod

when a wire carrying an electric current is placed horizontally across a line running north and south, the needle of a compass held under the wire will be deflected to the east. Ampère's work led to the invention of the *galvanometer*, which detects currents, and the telegraph.

The principles described by Ampère are used today in the operation of radio, television, electric motors, and other equipment. The unit of flow of an electric current was named the *ampere* to honor Ampère for his work.

ALSO READ: ELECTRICITY, MAGNET.

AMPHETAMINE see ADDICTION, DRUGS AND DRUG ABUSE.

AMPHIBIAN Animals that spend part of their lives in water and part on land are called amphibians. Usually, they hatch from eggs laid in streams or ponds. As adults, they move to land to live. The word "amphibian" comes from a Greek word that means "leading a double life."

The animals in the class Amphibia are placed by scientists midway between fishes and reptiles in the animal kingdom. They probably developed millions of years ago from fish that stayed out of water for longer and longer periods. The first amphibians were the pioneers for all backboned land animals. None of the early amphibians exists today. Most forms of

▲ *An amoeba moves by first putting out a "false foot" or pseudopod. The rest of the animal follows behind.*

▲ *Ampère was a pioneer of electricity and magnetism.*

◄ *Amphibians, such as the frog, are creatures that are at home both on dry land and in the water.*

Ichthyostega

Hylonomus

Common toad

Common frog

Frogs and toads look similar. You can tell a frog (right) by its moist, shiny skin. A toad (above) has a dry, rougher skin. Also, frogs hop farther than toads.

▲ *These are some of the first amphibians. They developed from fish that came out of the water to feed on the increasing amount of plant food on land. This was about 250 million years ago.*

amphibians died out altogether. Those that survived evolved into the frogs, toads, and salamanders we know today.

Although they breathe air, almost all amphibians must return to the water to lay their eggs. The young amphibians, called *larvae* (tadpoles or polliwogs), hatch in the water. They breathe by means of gills (like fish) and swim, using their tails as paddles. As they grow, they go through a *metamorphosis*, or change. They usually lose their gills and tails, grow legs, and begin breathing with their lungs. Then, like their parents, they

are able to live on land. Some salamanders breed on dry land, where they give birth to their young.

Amphibians usually have legs and a moist skin, which may be soft and smooth or rough and gritty. Unlike reptiles, amphibians do not have scales on their skin, and their toes are without claws.

There are two main kinds of amphibians—those with tails as adults and those without. All amphibians have tails when they are babies. Some kinds (such as frogs) lose their tails as they grow, but others (such as salamanders) keep them. Salamanders have long bodies, tails, and short stubby legs. Some kinds of very primitive amphibians with tails but no legs are called *caecilians*. Caecilians spend their lives either in water or burrowing in warm, moist earth. They look like earthworms.

A toad has stubbier legs than a frog, and its body is usually wider and flatter. A frog has smooth skin. A toad has rough skin, which often feels lumpy to the touch because of glands that make it look warty.

Amphibians have eyes similar to those of mammals. But they probably do not see very well. They have nostrils, but it is doubtful that they have a good sense of smell. They do not have visible ears, yet they do have eardrums—below and behind their eyes.

Most amphibians make their homes near freshwater ponds and lakes, or in damp places on land. Many amphibians hibernate during the winter in cool climates. When an amphibian senses danger, it either stays still, blending in with its surroundings, or it runs away. Some amphibians have skin glands that produce an irritating substance as a defense. If a hungry fish or some other animal bites the tail of a salamander, the salamander grows a new tail. Regrowth of a body part, such as a tail, is called *regeneration*. Many amphibians are helpful to humans, because they eat insect pests.

■ LEARN BY DOING

You can keep one or two frog or toad tadpoles in a home aquarium. Put rocks and soil at one end of the aquarium and water from a pond at the other. Put the tadpole in the water. Feed it once each day with lettuce, watercress, or plants from the pond where you found it.

In a few weeks, the tail of the tadpole will begin to shrink. You will see its legs start to form. Lungs will take over from the gills. Soon, the frog or toad will venture onto land.

Write notes to record the animal's development. Then release the young frog or toad in the country or a park near the water where you found the tadpole. It can then grow, and breed, so there will be more tadpoles next spring. ■

ALSO READ: AQUARIUM, FROGS AND TOADS, METAMORPHOSIS, REPTILE, SALAMANDER, TERRARIUM, VERTEBRATE.

▲ *The tree frog has long, padded toes that cling to leaves and tree branches. See how well it blends in with the leaves.*

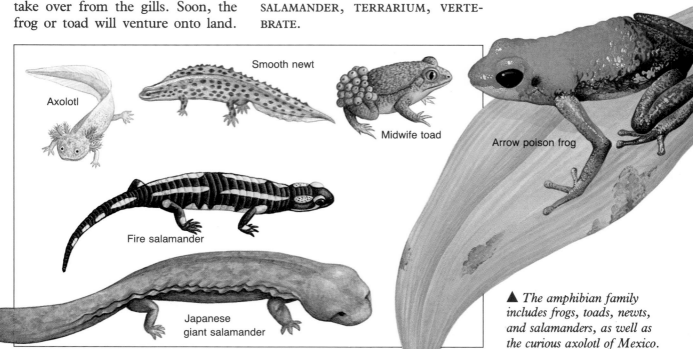

Smooth newt

Axolotl

Midwife toad

Arrow poison frog

Fire salamander

Japanese giant salamander

▲ *The amphibian family includes frogs, toads, newts, and salamanders, as well as the curious axolotl of Mexico.*

▲ *Amsterdam prospered in the 17th century because of overseas trade. These merchants' homes in the city were built at this time. Canals are a feature of Amsterdam.*

▼ *Roald Amundsen, first explorer to reach the South Pole.*

AMSTERDAM In the city of Amsterdam, in the Netherlands (Holland), there are more than 50 canals and over 400 bridges. No wonder travelers who visit Amsterdam call it the "Venice of the North" for, like Venice, this is a city of canals. Amsterdam is a city built in, on, and around water. It stands on a dike, or dam, on the Amstel River. Even the Royal Palace rests on thousands of wooden piles placed there in 1650. The modern buildings in Amsterdam rest on strong concrete piles that go deep into the sandy soil.

Amsterdam is the capital of the Netherlands, but government affairs are conducted in another city, The Hague. Amsterdam is a major European port and banking center. It is also a center of the diamond-cutting industry. Amsterdam was the home of the famous 17th-century artist Rembrandt van Rijn, commonly known as Rembrandt. Many of his paintings are owned by the city's Rijksmuseum.

Amsterdam became a city long before Columbus sailed for the New World. People still use buildings that date back to 1300. After the Netherlands won independence from Spain in the 1500's, Amsterdam became one of the great cities of Europe. In its early days, the city of New York was called New Amsterdam.

ALSO READ: NETHERLANDS, REMBRANDT VAN RIJN.

AMUNDSEN, ROALD (1872–1928) The first person to reach the South Pole was Roald Amundsen, a Norwegian explorer. Amundsen was born in Borge, near Oslo, Norway. He attended the University of Christiania and then joined the Norwegian navy.

Amundsen made a three-year expedition in the Arctic beginning in 1903. He was the first to navigate the Northwest Passage, a northern water route from the Atlantic to the Pacific. But Amundsen's greatest voyage began in 1910, at the other end of the Earth.

He intended to go to the North Pole, but he heard that Robert Peary had already reached it. So instead Amundsen headed to the South Pole in his ship, *Fram*. He learned that a British expedition, led by Robert F. Scott, was also on its way there.

Amundsen reached Antarctica in January, 1911. He and his men had to wait out the bitter cold, windy winter on the edge of the ice before they could head for the South Pole. In October (Antarctica's spring), they set out, with 52 well-trained dogs to pull their sledges. On the way to the Pole, they climbed glaciers, went around huge cracks in the ice, and survived freezing blizzards. Finally, on December 14, 1911, Amundsen placed the Norwegian flag at the South Pole. Scott and his men found the flag there when they reached the Pole a month after Amundsen's party.

Amundsen died in the Arctic, 17 years later. He disappeared while making an air search for another explorer, Umberto Nobile.

ALSO READ: ANTARCTICA; ARCTIC; NORTH POLE; NORTHWEST PASSAGE; SCOTT, ROBERT F.

ANATOMY
Anatomy is the study of how living things—plants, animals, and people—are built. The word comes from the Greek meaning "to cut up."

Cutting apart or *dissecting* dead human bodies was a crime in ancient times. In the 1st century A.D., Galen, a Greek doctor, dissected animals to study their parts. His writings on anatomy remained important until the 1400's. Andreas Vesalius, a Belgian doctor, wrote a famous book on anatomy in 1543. It was based on his dissections of dead human bodies.

There are several branches of anatomy. *Gross anatomy* is the study of large parts of the body. *Histology* is the study of tissue, and *cytology* is the study of cells. *Comparative anatomy* deals with differences in structure.

ALSO READ: BIOLOGY, HUMAN BODY.

ANCIENT CIVILIZATIONS
Many civilizations have grown up and disappeared in places all over the world. The ancient civilization that most affected the development of the Western World was that which grew up around the Mediterranean Sea. It started with the Sumerian civilization more than 5,000 years ago and ended with the fall of the Western Roman Empire in A.D. 476.

There were other ancient, and impressive civilizations in China, India, Africa, and North and South America. The contributions of these peoples to the way people of the Western World live today are not so easily traced.

Thousands of years ago, people everywhere lived in small groups, or tribes. Almost everyone in a group worked at hunting animals and gathering wild plants for food. Tribes roamed all over, searching for food. This *nomadic* (wandering) life went on until some people discovered that they could *plant* seeds and raise crops. Then they *domesticated* (tamed) animals, to keep for food (sheep, goats, cattle), and to help as beasts of burden (asses, camels, horses).

The first cities developed in areas that were especially good for farming. On a farm, so much food could be raised that not everyone had to work to provide the next meal. People worked as full-time priests, government officials, soldiers, craftsmen, merchants, artists, and musicians. Life became very complex. Writing was developed to help people conduct the business of their cities.

The Gifts of Ancient Civilizations
WRITING. With the invention of writing, people could make lasting records of their laws, religions, folk tales, poetry, and business deals. The

▲ *Anatomy owes much to Vesalius, the first great anatomist. He made careful drawings, like the one above, of the human body.*

▼ *An ancient Sumerian village probably looked much like this. The huts were made of marsh reeds, just like these in Iraq today.*

ANCIENT CIVILIZATIONS

Civilization and Location	Dates	What Did They Achieve?	Famous Cities	Why Did They Decline?
Sumerians lived between the Tigris and Euphrates rivers in what is now Iraq.	3500 B.C. — 2000 B.C.	First people to develop word-writing, before 3000 B.C. Called *cuneiform* (wedge-shaped) writing, written on lumps of clay.	Kish, Lagash, Ur	Were conquered. But their art and architecture were so good that the invaders learned and copied from them. Babylonia later developed out of Sumeria.
Egyptians lived along the Nile River.	3100 B.C. — 525 B.C.	Built huge temples and large tombs called pyramids out of stone. Invented another form of word-writing called *hieroglyphics*.	Memphis, Thebes, Akhetaton, Alexandria	Rebellions and invasions weakened the empire. Finally, conquered by the Kushites.
Minoans lived on the island of Crete near Greece.	3000 B.C. — 1100 B.C.	Made pottery and wall paintings full of bright, gay patterns. Built large outdoor theaters and loved to watch outdoor sports.	Knossos, Phaestos	Fell as Greece grew in power. Earthquakes may have speeded their end.
Indus Valley Peoples lived in what is now Pakistan.	2500 B.C. — 1500 B.C.	Famous for their well-planned cities with neat blocks of buildings facing paved streets. Sewers ran under many of the streets. Fine craftsmen worked in the cities.	Harappa, Mohenjo-Daro	Vast floods damaged the cities. Invaders from the west probably conquered the people of the valley.
Hittites lived along the Halys Rivers in what is now Turkey.	1900 B.C. — 1200 B.C.	Probably the first people to make things out of iron.	Hattusas	Allies of the Hittites rebelled. The Hittite city-states gradually lost power.
Babylonians lived between the Tigris and Euphrates rivers in what is now Iraq.	1900 B.C. — 538 B.C.	Great lawmakers. The Code of Hammurabi is one of the oldest known sets of written law. Even trade was governed by law. There were many scientists and mathematicians. They were the first people to count seconds and minutes by 60's.	Babylon	Conquered by the Persians in 538 B.C.
Phoenicians lived along eastern coast of the Mediterranean.	1100 B.C. — 842 B.C.	Invented an alphabet improved by the Greeks and used in the west today. Very skillful in making cloth and other goods. Traded in many parts of the world.	Byblos, Tyre, Sidon, Ugarit	Cities grew weaker as Assyria grew in power and took over most of the region.
Chou Dynasty China	1027 B.C. — 256 B.C.	Iron tools replaced bronze. Literature and the visual arts reached great heights. Confucius and Lao-tse, great philosophers and teachers, lived at this time.	Peking, Chungking	Generals and politicians argued with each other. China broke up into small, warring states.
Hebrews were originally nomadic. Lived at various times in what is now Israel and Jordan.	1000 B.C. — 587 B.C.	Created a great literature. Most important was the Old Testament of the Bible, the books of which were probably written between about 900 B.C. and 150 B.C. King Solomon, a well-known king of Israel, built a great temple in Jerusalem.	Jerusalem, Hebron	The Babylonians conquered the Hebrews and destroyed the great temple in Jerusalem.
Assyrians lived along the Tigris River in what is now Iraq.	800 B.C. — 612 B.C.	Formed the first great army with iron weapons. This helped them to win many battles.	Assur, Nineveh	Conquered by the Babylonians.
Greeks lived in the southern part of what is now Greece.	800 B.C. — 197 B.C.	Built fine buildings and sculptures. Wrote great poetry and drama. Had many wise scientists and philosophers. Democracy began in Greece.	Athens, Sparta, Thebes, Corinth	The Roman Empire was gaining strength taking away trade and turning farmers into soldiers. Rome finally conquered Greece.
Romans spread from the city of Rome west to England and east to Mesopotamia. At its height, included all lands around the Mediterranean.	735 B.C. — A.D. 476	Excellent administrators, first to control a vast area from a central place and still let cities govern themselves. Used their army to build bridges and roads to improve the lives of conquered peoples.	Rome, Pompeii, Byzantium	Civil war and political assassinations tore the Roman Empire apart. The empire split in half in A.D. 395. The western Romans became easy prey for invaders. The eastern empire continued until A.D. 1453.
Kushites lived in Africa along the Nile River, south of Egypt. Expanded through much of Africa below Sahara desert.	725 B.C. — A.D. 350	The city of Meroe became a great, iron-making center. Made beautiful pottery, built pyramids, temples, and palaces. Developed a written language not yet deciphered.	Meroe, Napata	Conquered by their neighbors, the Ethiopians.
Persians lived in an area from the Indus River to the Aegean Sea at the height of the empire.	700 B.C. — 331 B.C.	Built huge palaces of mud, brick, and stone. Beasts of legend appeared in their wall paintings and sculptures. Mail was delivered by "Pony Express."	Persepolis	The Persian Empire crumbled before the army of Alexander the Great in 331 B.C.

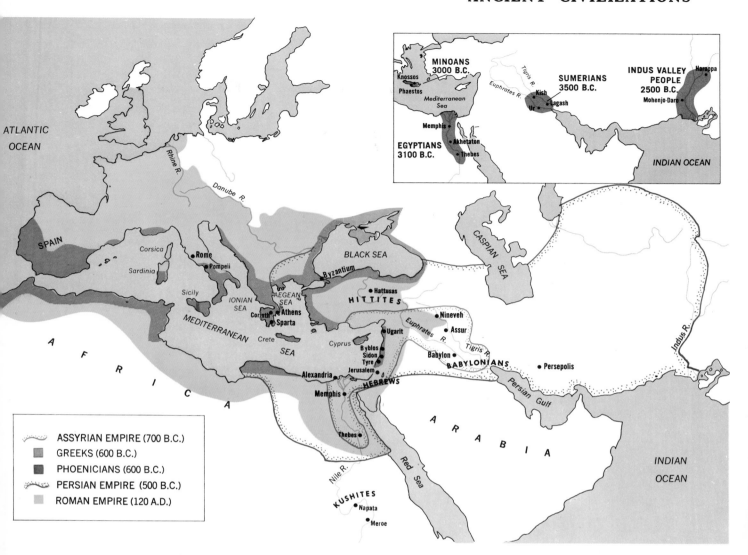

Sumerians were the first people to develop word writing, more than 5,000 years ago. Before the Sumerians, if a writer wanted to say "9 cows," he had to draw 9 small pictures of cows. A Sumerian writer simply wrote the word-character for "cow" and the number-symbol for "9." This Sumerian writing is called *cuneiform* (wedge-shaped) because characters were scratched into soft clay tablets with a wedge-shaped stick.

The Egyptians, about 3000 B.C., developed a writing system called *hieroglyphics*, or "sacred carving." Hieroglyphics were first chiseled into stone monuments, but later they were written with pen and ink. Like cuneiform, hieroglyphics was word writing, but the characters were different because they were not made with a wedge-shaped stick. Both systems later added new characters for syllable sounds. Many hundreds of years later, people who lived on the eastern shores of the Mediterranean Sea invented the first alphabets.

MEDICINE AND SCIENCE. The Egyptians had highly skilled doctors who understood the human body. The Greeks, too, had good doctors. Hippocrates, a Greek doctor who lived 400 years before Christ, is called the "father of modern medicine." His ideas were the basis of modern medicine, which developed in the 1800's. The Greeks also had many famous mathematicians, and scientists, such as Euclid and Archimedes.

▼ *People in Mesopotamia used seals, like this one, instead of signing letters.*

▲ *The Great Sphinx and the pyramid of the Pharaoh Cheops at Giza, Egypt. These huge structures were built in the desert and have defied the passing of time.*

LITERATURE. People continue to read and enjoy the literature of the ancient Greeks. Homer's epic poems, the *Iliad* and the *Odyssey*, are great literature, as are the plays of Sophocles, Aeschylus, Euripides, and Aristophanes. From the Romans came the magnificent poetry of Ovid, Horace, and Virgil. The Bible, a book of sacred scriptures, is also great literature. It contains much ancient history and is the foundation of Jewish and Christian religious beliefs. Other world religions also produced ancient holy books.

PHILOSOPHY. Greek philosophers wondered about the nature of the universe. Others thought about conduct. The works of many Greek philosophers, including Socrates, Plato, and Aristotle, are still studied today. Chinese thinkers also wondered about such questions. The writings of Confucius and Lao-tse are still studied.

SCULPTURE, PAINTING, AND ARCHITECTURE. The ancient civilizations produced marvelous works of art. The Egyptians honored their pharaohs with enormous statues, tombs, and temples. Their stone pyramids were built to last for thousands of years, and to stand boldly against the desert sands. You can still see colorful scenes painted on the walls in many of their ornate tombs. On the Mediterranean island of Crete, the Minoan civilization lasted from about 3000 to 1100 B.C. The Minoans built huge palaces, painted, and made

beautiful pottery. About the same time, the ancient Chinese made handsome bronze ritual vessels.

Ancient Greek temples are among the most magnificent buildings in history. The Greeks were also interested in the human body and produced some of the world's best sculpture of the human form. Roman sculptors copied many of their statues from the Greeks, but they also made some remarkably handsome portrait sculpture. They built large, airy buildings with huge arches, vaults, and domed roofs. They also built countless bridges, roads, dams, and waterways.

LAW AND DEMOCRACY. The idea that people should be ruled by a written *code* (set) of laws, and not by the whims of rulers, began in ancient times. One of the first and most famous codes of law came from Mesopotamia. King Hammurabi of Babylon, who lived almost 4,000 years ago, had laws carved on a stone column. The *Code of Hammurabi* may seem harsh to many today, but Babylonians who broke the law knew

their crime and knew what their punishment might be.

The Greeks believed that the citizens should decide the laws. They called this form of government *democracy*, which means, "rule by the people." The Romans added to the Greek laws. Many law codes of modern Western nations are based partly on these ancient codes, and some of the principles of modern democratic government are derived from the Greek and Roman systems.

Mysteries from the Past Historians know that northern tribes invaded Rome in A.D. 476, thus ending the Western Roman Empire. Before this, Rome had taken over the Greeks' territory, and earlier still the Greeks had defeated the mighty Persian empire. But other ancient civilizations left almost no clue as to why they disappeared. For example, the Minoan empire crumbled after 1400 B.C., when all its towns and palaces burned. No one knows why.

Scientists called *archeologists* search

Money was not used in ancient Egypt. Everyone was paid in goods, usually food. This food was taken from the farmers as a tax.

Several times during the Twentieth Egyptian Dynasty the workmen building a tomb for the pharaoh were not paid their food on time. They went on strike. The men marched to the temple where supplies were kept and sat down outside calling for bread. They soon got what they wanted because it was unthinkable that the pharaoh's tomb should not be finished.

The ancient Egyptians farmed fields alongside the Nile. Here you can see farmers cutting wheat and carrying it to be threshed. They are using oxen and donkeys as beasts of burden. Harvesting was done twice a year.

▲ *This* stela *or stone slab is engraved with the laws of Hammurabi the Great, ruler of Babylon from 1728 to 1686* B.C.

▶ *A Chinese craftsman made this figure of a juggler balancing a bear. The ancient Chinese loved circus acts.*

the sites of ancient cities for walls, broken pieces of sculpture, pottery, cooking tools, and other clues to the lives of long-ago peoples. Yet hundreds of mysteries and unanswered questions remain about each ancient civilization.

■ LEARN BY DOING

Study the table, which lists several of the famous ancient civilizations, what we remember them for, their famous cities, and reasons for the end of each civilization. Imagine you are a

writer filling in this table 2,000 years from now. What would you say about our present civilization? ■

For further information on:
Architecture, *see* ABU SIMBEL, ACROPOLIS, ARCHEOLOGY, GREAT WALL OF CHINA, PARTHENON, PYRAMID, SEVEN WONDERS OF THE WORLD, STONEHENGE.
Art, *see* ART HISTORY, GREEK ART, ORIENTAL ART, ROMAN ART, SPHINX.
Leaders of Long Ago, *see* ALARIC; ALEXANDER THE GREAT; CAESAR,

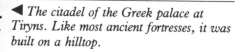

▼ *The Greeks were famous for their pottery, which they decorated with scenes from myths and from everyday life. This water jar shows women at a fountain.*

◀ *The citadel of the Greek palace at Tiryns. Like most ancient fortresses, it was built on a hilltop.*

ANDERSEN, HANS CHRISTIAN

(1805–1875) Once upon a time, in Denmark, a boy dreamed and played with his puppets. The neighborhood children laughed at him, and adults said he was a fool. But he grew up to become one of the most famous and best-loved writers of all time. He was Hans Christian Andersen.

Andersen was born in the village of Odense. His father was a shoemaker, and his mother washed clothes to earn money. His father would read to the boy on cold winter evenings, sometimes from *The Arabian Nights*. His father died when Andersen was 11 years old. Hans had to give up school. He went to Copenhagen three years later, with only a little money from his savings. He was determined to become famous.

He tried very hard to be an actor, singer, or dancer in Copenhagen, but he almost starved. Then a director of the Royal Theater befriended him. Andersen was given a scholarship so he could finish his education. Going back to school was difficult for him because he was older than the other students.

Andersen's first fairy tales were published in 1835. In all, he wrote 168 stories. He was sensitive and kind, and he fell in love three times, but he never married. His fairy tales brought him the fame for which he had yearned, and he went on writing them until 1872. He also wrote novels, plays, and poems.

The stories that Hans Christian Andersen wrote are not just for children. They are for people of all ages, in all times. "The Little Mermaid" is one of the saddest and also one of the most loved of his stories. "The Em-

▲ *The ruins of Pompeii, as they are today. This Roman town was buried by falling ash and lava when the volcano Vesuvius erupted in* A.D. *79.*

▲ *Hans Christian Andersen, Danish storyteller.*

▲ *The Little Mermaid statue in Copenhagen harbor. The statue is a memorial to Hans Christian Andersen, one of whose best-loved stories was called "The Little Mermaid."*

peror's New Clothes" is a happier tale, and so are "The Princess and the Pea," and "The Ugly Duckling." Most of these tales have a moral, or lesson. Things that Andersen loved as a child appear in his stories. His mother's garden is the garden of "The Snow Queen." His grandmother told him the tale that became "The Tinderbox."

The fairy tales of Hans Christian Andersen have been translated into over 80 languages. They have been made into movies, plays, ballets, and puppet shows. In Copenhagen harbor stands a statue, *The Little Mermaid*, the Danes' memorial to Hans Andersen, who once said, "Life is the most wonderful fairy tale of all."

ALSO READ: FAIRY TALE.

ANDERSON, MARIAN (born 1902)

Marian Anderson was six years old when she first sang in public, in the choir of the Union Baptist Church in Philadelphia, her home city. She later became one of the world's greatest singers.

Marian Anderson's parents were poor. Her church helped to pay for singing lessons. After years of voice training, she entered a contest to sing with the New York Philharmonic

▼ *Marian Anderson, distinguished singer.*

Orchestra and won first place out of 300 contestants.

She went to Europe, where her concerts thrilled many people. But she was not allowed to sing in Constitution Hall in Washington, D.C., in 1939, because she was black. Mrs. Franklin D. Roosevelt invited her to sing on the steps of the Lincoln Memorial instead. She gave a memorable, free concert there on Easter Sunday, 1939.

In 1955, Marian Anderson became the first black to sing with the Metropolitan Opera Company in New York. She later sang at the White House. Her rich-textured contralto voice was at its best singing Negro Spirituals. She picked the title of one spiritual, "My Lord, What a Morning," as the title of her autobiography. She has received many honors, including the Spingarn Medal and the Presidential Medal of Freedom.

ALSO READ: SINGING.

ANDES MOUNTAINS

The Andes curve like a vast wall down the western side of South America. They form the longest mountain chain in the world, at about 5,500 miles (8,900 km). Only the Himalaya Mountains of Asia rise higher. Forty-two Andean peaks are taller than Mount McKinley, North America's tallest mountain. The highest peak in the Andes and in the Western Hemisphere is Aconcagua, in Argentina. It rises 22,834 feet (6,960 m).

Fingers of the Andes almost touch the Caribbean Sea in the north. Three separate ranges come together in Colombia. The Andes then continue south through Ecuador and Peru and become widest in Bolivia. The range disappears into the ocean at the tip of South America. Some evidence shows the range continues in Antarctica. (See the map with the article on SOUTH AMERICA.)

The Andes region is one of fire and

ice. Many active volcanoes show that these mountains are still being formed. Earthquakes sometimes shake the area. Great glaciers, warmed by the sun, can slide down valleys.

Spanish explorers looked for the Incas' source of gold in the Andes in the 1500's. Many other valuable mineral ores have been found and mined there in modern times. Hardy Andean Indians still live simply high up in these mountains.

ALSO READ: INCA, MOUNTAIN, SOUTH AMERICA.

ANDORRA The tiny country of Andorra lies high in the Pyrenees Mountains between France and Spain. (See the map with the article on SPAIN.) Catalan, which is somewhat like French and Spanish, is the language of Andorra.

Fall is a busy season in Andorra, because the farmers must get ready for a long, hard winter. The capital city, Andorra la Vella, is a colorful sight, with ancient stone houses, shops, and modern hotels. Tourism has become an important industry. Thousands of tourists arrive to look at the beautiful countryside and also to buy inexpensive goods. There is no sales tax in Andorra.

Charlemagne, emperor of the Holy Roman Empire, gave this tiny country its independence in the 700's, as a

reward to the Andorrans for helping him in battle. An arrangement was made in 1278 for two co-princes to rule Andorra. The co-princes today are the Bishop of Urgel in Spain and the President of France. Andorra pays these rulers a small tribute. In return, the princes manage the courts and police. But Andorra governs its own affairs by a General Council of 24 members elected every 4 years.

ALSO READ: CHARLEMAGNE, EUROPE.

▲ *The Andes Mountains, the second highest range in the world, were the last stronghold of the Incas.*

ANDORRA

Capital City: Andorra la Vella (15,700 people).
Area: 175 square miles (453 sq. km).
Population: 55,000.
Government: Principality.
Main Products: Tourism, postage stamps.
Unit of Money: French franc and Spanish peseta.
Official Language: Catalan. (Spanish and French are also spoken.)

▲ *Within the constellation, or star pattern, of Andromeda is a cluster of stars called the Andromeda galaxy.*

Before anesthetics were commonly used in operations, circus acts entertained American audiences with a "grand exhibition of laughing gas." The gas was guaranteed to make those who inhaled it "laugh, sing, dance, or fight."

ANDROMEDA The story of Andromeda is one of the myths of ancient Greece. Andromeda was the daughter of Cepheus and Cassiopeia, king and queen of Ethiopia.

Cassiopeia was very vain. She boasted that Andromeda was as beautiful as the nymphs of Poseidon, god of the sea. Her boasting made Poseidon very angry, so he sent a horrible sea monster to attack Ethiopia. To save their kingdom, the king and queen chained Andromeda to a rock and left her for the monster.

The hero Perseus saw her and instantly fell in love with her. He killed the monster and carried off Andromeda to marry her. After her death, the gods turned Andromeda into a constellation of stars in the sky. At the heart of the Andromeda constellation shines a beautiful galaxy.

ALSO READ: GODS AND GODDESSES, MYTHOLOGY, PERSEUS.

ANEMOMETER see WIND.

ANESTHETICS Doctors sometimes need to do something to a patient that may hurt. They give the patient a drug called an anesthetic, which keeps the patient from feeling pain. "Anesthetic" comes from two Greek words meaning "without feeling." A *general* anesthetic makes a patient unconscious. A *local* anesthetic stops all feeling in one part of the patient's body. Novocain, for example, is a local anesthetic that a dentist injects into the patient's gums so he or she does not feel any pain.

Before the discovery of modern anesthetics, patients drank wine or took drugs to make them sleepy before operations. Modern anesthetics were not discovered until the 1800's.

Dr. Crawford Williamson Long of Jefferson, Georgia, first used a chemical called *ether* as an anesthetic in December, 1842. Three months later he used it when he removed a tumor from a patient's neck. Records show he charged 25 cents for the ether.

A Connecticut dentist named

▼ *William Morton of Boston began using ether as an anesthetic in 1846.*

Horace Wells, in 1844, had patients sniff *nitrous oxide* before a tooth was pulled. This mild anesthetic, which is still in use, does not put a person completely to sleep. It is called "laughing gas," because it makes people feel happy and giggly while feeling no pain.

Meanwhile, a Boston dentist, Dr. William Morton, was also trying ether. He persuaded a surgeon, Dr. John Warren, to let him give a patient some ether to breathe before an operation in 1846. Dr. Warren was doubtful, but the patient went quietly to sleep. The astonished Dr. Warren exclaimed to a group of doctors who were watching, "Gentlemen, this is no humbug!"

Dr. James Young Simpson, a Scotsman, gave an anesthetic called *chloroform* to a woman to breathe just before she gave birth to a baby in 1847. In 1853, Queen Victoria of Britain asked for chloroform when she gave birth to her seventh child. Anesthetics became popular after that.

When people have an operation today, they can remain unconscious through it. People feel pain through the nerves of their bodies. General anesthetics work on the central nervous system. These drugs prevent the sensation of pain being recognized by the brain.

Patients may be given some medication to relax them before an operation. Then an intravenous (into a vein) injection of an anesthetic makes the patient lose consciousness. An *anesthesiologist* (a doctor who gives anesthetics) continues to give anesthetic gas to keep the patient unconscious until the surgeon has finished the operation.

ALSO READ: DRUGS AND DRUG ABUSE, MEDICINE, NERVOUS SYSTEM, SURGERY.

ANGLE Two straight lines meet at a point to form an angle. The point where the lines meet is called the *vertex* of the angle. If the lines make a square corner, they form a *right angle*. A street corner is often a right angle. An angle smaller than a right angle is called *acute*. An angle larger than a right angle is called *obtuse*. The size of an angle is measured in units called *degrees*. A full circle contains 360 degrees (the symbol ° stands for degrees).

■ LEARN BY DOING

Draw the face of a clock. It is a circle, so it has 360°. Attach hands to the clock using a straight pin and two long strips of paper. Point one hand at 12 and the other at 3. The hands form a right angle of 90° (one-fourth of 360°). Move the hand from 3 to 6. This does not look like an angle. But it is called a *straight angle*, and it contains 180°. Now move the hand from 6 to 8. Is this angle obtuse? How many degrees are there in this angle? If you are not sure, here is a clue—there are 30° between each five minutes on the clock face. Now try to form an angle that has 150°. ■

ALSO READ: GEOMETRY.

ANGLO-SAXONS Anglo-Saxon peoples from northern Europe invaded Britain over 1,500 years ago. They included Angles, Saxons, and Jutes, and they began to settle in Britain after its Roman rulers had left in the 5th century. The invading people drove away the native Britons westward, and formed their own kingdoms, including Northumbria, Mercia, and Wessex. The most famous king of Wessex was Alfred the Great. The Anglo-Saxons gave the name *Englalond* (England) to their new land and ruled there until King Harold was defeated in the Norman Conquest of 1066.

ALSO READ: ALFRED THE GREAT, ENGLISH HISTORY, ENGLISH LANGUAGE.

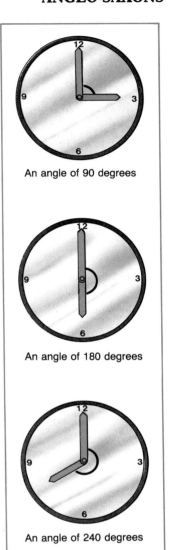

An angle of 90 degrees

An angle of 180 degrees

An angle of 240 degrees

It is sometimes difficult to make an exact right angle. An easy way is to fold a piece of paper in half and then fold it a second time along the crease. You have a perfect right angle.

ANGOLA The country that today is the Republic of Angola was inhabited by African Bushmen and Bantu tribes until a Portuguese navigator, Diogo Cão, claimed the region for Portugal in 1482. The Portuguese developed the slave trade in the 16th century. For a brief time, 1641–1648, the Dutch took control of the region and the slave trade.

In the 1800's, Portugal tried unsuccessfully to gain territory in Africa's interior. Portugal hoped to connect Angola, then known as Portuguese West Africa, with another colony, Mozambique, known as Portuguese East Africa. Britain, however, forced Portugal out of the interior.

About 400,000 Portuguese settlers immigrated to Angola during the first half of the 20th century. They developed industries and hydroelectric power. Oil was discovered near Luanda, the capital, in 1955.

The black Angolans, however, rebelled against the repressive Portuguese rule. Fighting broke out in 1960 and Portugal rushed in troops. A 15-year struggle for independence began. In 1972, Portugal changed Angola from an overseas province to an autonomous (self-governing) state, and in 1975 granted it full independence.

A fierce struggle for supremacy was waged among rival factions, with the Soviet-backed Popular Movement (MPLA) gaining control of the gov-

▲ *Angola's capital is the seaport city of Luanda.*

ernment in 1976. The moderate National Union (UNITA) resisted this takeover, fighting a civil war through the 1980's, with Cuban and South African troops involved. Efforts are being made to ensure the withdrawal of all foreign forces.

Angola's land rises sharply beyond the narrow coastal plain, into a high plateau of forests and grasslands. The climate is suitable for growing coffee, cotton, corn, sugar, and sisal. Mines in Angola produce diamonds, iron, and copper. Oil is an important export. Angola's industries include cereal mills, fish and palm oil processing plants, and foundries.

ALSO READ: AFRICA, PORTUGAL.

ANGOLA

Capital City: Luanda (1,200,000 people).
Area: 481,388 square miles (1,246,700 sq. km).
Population: 9,000,000.
Government: Republic.
Main Products: Coffee, diamonds, oil.
Unit of Money: Kwanza.
Official Language: Portuguese.

ANIMAL What is an animal? You might think that's a silly question. You know a monkey when you see one. And anyone can tell a goose from a gooseberry, or a dog from a dogwood tree. But there are some animals that don't look anything like the animals familiar to most people. The sea cucumber has no head or tail. Its body looks like a cucumber. And it certainly doesn't look like an elephant. But the goose, dog, sea cucumber, and elephant are only four of about a million different kinds of animals.

All animals have certain things in common. They are all made of cells that are different from plant cells. They all can move, even if only for a part of their lives. And they all must take in food as a source of energy.

All living things are made up of tiny building blocks of living matter called *cells*. The cells of an animal have a baglike outer covering, called a *membrane*. The cell is soft, like a tiny balloon full of juice. It is in the cell that the activities that mean "life" happen. A cell takes in food, water, and oxygen, uses them to produce energy, and then gives off waste products. An animal can consist of a single cell that does all these things. An amoeba, for example, is a one-celled animal that lives in ponds. More complicated animals are made of larger numbers of cells. Many millions of cells working together make up the human animal.

The pressure of the atmosphere on Earth could flatten animal cells. But animals have adapted to certain ways of living or certain forms that prevent their being squashed. For example, one-celled animals always live in water, which helps the cell hold its shape. The water may be a pond, an ocean, or the fluid in a bigger animal's body. Other animals have developed outside coverings (shells) or inside supports (bones) that protect and shape them. The hard shell on a

INVERTEBRATES

Sea cucumber
(echinoderm)

Butterfly (insect)

VERTEBRATES

Eel (fish)

Anaconda snake
(reptile)

Chimpanzee (mammal)

Seal
(mammal)

Rhinoceros
(mammal)

Flamingo
(bird)

ANIMAL

▶ *The fierce little weasel will attack animals larger than itself.*

The koala is perhaps the most fussy eater of all the animals. It lives only on the leaves of eucalyptus trees—and only on the leaves of five out of the 350 species of eucalyptus at that!

beetle is an outside protection, as is the "skin," called *cuticle*, of an earthworm. The skeleton of a bird or fish is an inside bony support.

At some time in its life, every animal is able to move its body. This is called locomotion. Most animals move all their lives. A sponge has a swimming "childhood," but spends its adult life attached to a rock.

Part of the ability of an animal to move is the ability to react to what is happening around it. Simple one-celled animals react to food by moving toward it and react to danger by moving away. Higher forms of animals, such as mammals and birds, can see, hear, smell, feel, and taste. They have nervous systems that allow them to sense what is happening,

then react quickly.

Animals are *consumers*. They have to *eat* in order to get energy to live. Plants produce their own food, using energy directly from the sun. Animals get the sun's energy as a "hand-me-down" by eating plants or by eating other animals that have eaten plants. Every animal has adapted to its own way of getting its share of the sun's energy. This is one reason for the fantastic variety of animal life.

■ LEARN BY DOING

You can find out a lot about animals by reading the articles listed below. You can learn even more by getting out and looking around you. Watch the activity in the cracks of an old sidewalk. Lift up a fallen tree

▲ *The male Adélie penguin offers a female a pebble. If she accepts, they build a nest of stones.*

▶ *A mountain lion or puma, a big cat of North America.*

branch and see how many creatures scuttle quickly out of sight. Watch, listen, and wonder. ■

For further information on:

Animal Defenses, *see* CLAWS AND NAILS, HANDS AND FEET, HORNS AND ANTLERS, PROTECTIVE COLORING.

Animal Life, *see* AGRICULTURE, ANIMAL FAMILIES, ANIMAL HOMES, ANIMAL KINGDOM, ANIMAL MOVEMENT, DOMESTICATED ANIMALS, HIBERNATION, METAMORPHOSIS, MIGRATION.

Biology, *see* CELL, EGG, EMBRYO, EVOLUTION, GROWTH, LIFE, PROTIST, REPRODUCTION, SKELETON, ZOOLOGY.

Ecology, *see* ANIMAL DISTRIBUTION, ANIMAL HOMES, ECOLOGY, FOOD WEB, NATURE STUDY, PLANT DISTRIBUTION, ZOO.

▲ *The African elephant is the largest land animal.*

▲ *The koala of Australia is sometimes called a "bear," but it is not a true bear at all.*

▶ *The Arabian camel is adapted for desert life. It stores food as fat in its hump.*

▶ *The golden eagle, a large bird of prey, uses its hooked claws to seize its victim.*

If a worm is cut into pieces, each piece will form a complete new worm. More amazing is that if a worm is "trained" to find its way through a maze, then cut in half and allowed to regrow, both new worms will remember their way through the maze.

▼ *Defense by color-change. Flatfish can match their color to the seabed on which they lie.*

ANIMAL DEFENSES An animal needs to protect itself from its enemies. If its defenses are not good enough, it will not survive. Every creature has some kind of defense. The elephant has enormous size and strength. A deer has speed. An armadillo has an armor of thick, horny plates. A cat has claws. A butterfly flies in a zigzag way, making it difficult to catch.

At the first sign of danger, most animals try to escape. For some animals, this means running away as fast as they can. Antelopes, gazelles, and many other mammals that live in open country depend on speed. So do many fish, insects, and birds.

Many animals escape by hiding. The brightly colored little fish around coral reefs are an example. Each fish vanishes into its own hole in the coral when trouble comes. Some small land animals try to keep their enemies from seeing them by holding perfectly still in the tall grasses or bushes. Rabbits have been known to "freeze" in this way for half an hour or more.

Some animals are able to hide from their enemies because they match their surroundings. For example, an insect called the walking stick lives in trees and looks almost exactly like a small brown twig. Because of this, it is practically invisible to its enemies. The color of the skin or coat of desert animals, such as the horned toad and the desert rat, matches the sandy color of the desert.

Some fish can change their color to match different backgrounds. The flounder, for example, will turn a grayish-brown color if it is close to a sandy area under the water. Its back will even show little speckles that look like grains of sand. Other creatures change color when the seasons change. In winter, the Arctic fox and the weasel, a small animal that looks like a mink, change from brown to pure white, so they can hardly be seen against the snow.

Special armor is a way of hiding for some creatures. Certain armadillos are covered with thick plates. When they roll themselves into tight balls, enemies cannot get at their soft flesh. Turtles and tortoises have hard shells to guard their tender bodies. They pull their heads and legs quickly into the safety of their shells. Clams, oysters, and similar sea creatures have shells that snap shut.

Many animals have special ways to discourage attackers. Some play a game of "make believe" to fool their enemies. The hognose snake, a harmless, nonpoisonous creature, puts on a big show to scare off a would-be attacker. First it rears up and hisses, pretending to be ready to strike. If this does not succeed, the snake suddenly collapses and begins to twitch and roll about, as if in agony. Then it flops on its back, looking dead.

Other beasts drive away their enemies with unpleasant smells, or even with smoke screens. When a skunk is alarmed, special glands near its tail shoot off a spray with a terrible odor. Stink bugs can release foul-smelling gases to drive away birds. If trapped, most animals will fight, using whatever weapons they have—horns, hoofs, claws, teeth, or stingers.

■ LEARN BY DOING

Use this encyclopedia to help make a list of other animals and their defenses. People too had to defend themselves for thousands of years without the kinds of weapons there are today. Yet they survived. What ways might early people have used to defend themselves? ■

ALSO READ: ANIMAL MOVEMENT, CLAWS AND NAILS, HORNS AND ANT-LERS, PROTECTIVE COLORING, TEETH.

ANIMAL DISTRIBUTION Animals are found in every part of the Earth, both on land and in water. The world's oceans are filled with saltwater fish, shellfish, octopuses, sea mammals, and numerous other creatures. The freshwater rivers, lakes, and ponds are populated by similar kinds of animals. Land animals, including birds, are found on all continents and in all climates. Humans are probably the only land animals that can survive on any continent and in almost any climate. Other kinds of animals are suited only for certain kinds of living places.

Places of Cold and Heat The Antarctic is so icy and barren that people cannot live there for long. But penguins, seals, and whales are especially suited for polar life. They have heavy layers of fat under their skin to keep them warm, and they feed on the *plankton* (microscopic animal and plant life) and fish that abound in the Antarctic waters. In the Arctic, around the North Pole, the climate is

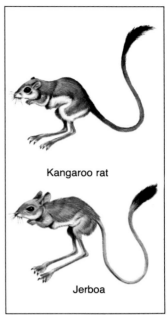

Kangaroo rat

Jerboa

▲ *Unrelated animals can look alike because they live in similar habitats. The kangaroo rat lives in North America. The jerboa comes from Africa. But both are designed the same way, for desert life.*

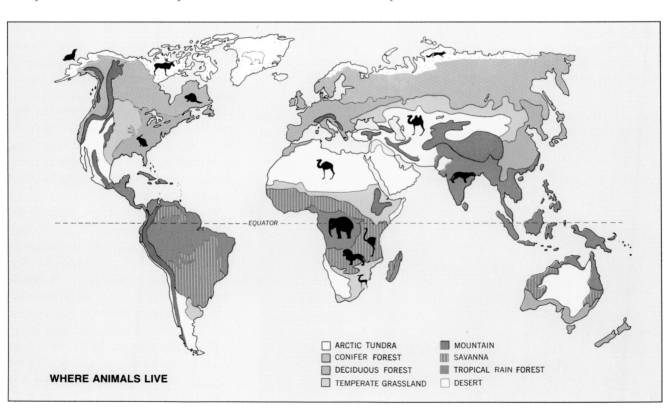

WHERE ANIMALS LIVE

— EQUATOR

☐ ARCTIC TUNDRA ▨ MOUNTAIN
▨ CONIFER FOREST ▥ SAVANNA
▨ DECIDUOUS FOREST ▨ TROPICAL RAIN FOREST
☐ TEMPERATE GRASSLAND ☐ DESERT

Marco Polo, the Venetian explorer who spent 17 years at the court of Kublai Khan in China in the late 1200's, reported that the Great Khan had a collection of leopards, lynxes, tigers, and other animals. They were mostly used for hunting.

not quite so harsh, but it is still cold and snowy much of the year. Many of the animals there, such as polar bears, Arctic foxes, lemmings, reindeer, and ermine, need thick coats of fur during the coldest months. The fur on some of these animals turns white in winter as protective coloring.

High mountains have living conditions similar to polar regions. So the animals of cold mountain tops also have heavy coats. Many of them—including the bighorn sheep of North America and the ibex, a wild goat of Asia—are also good at climbing the rocky cliffs.

Animals of deserts in Africa, Asia, North America, and Australia often have certain traits in common. Desert regions are very dry, and usually very hot. Many desert creatures are able to go for long periods without water. The kangaroo rat and the pocket mouse never drink water at all. They get enough water from the seeds and the plants that they eat. The dromedary, or one-humped camel, lives for long periods of time in the desert, where few plants grow. When it cannot get enough plant food, the animal's body uses the fat stored in its hump. Other desert animals include scorpions, jack rabbits, owls, lizards, and snakes. Some come out only at night, when it is cool.

Places in Between Most animals, however, do not need to cope with such extremes of heat and cold. The forests, jungles, and open grasslands of temperate (in-between) climates provide the right living conditions for many, many animals.

Some woodlands are *coniferous forests*, made up of cone-bearing trees. Coniferous forest is often called *taiga*. Taiga, mainly in northern regions, provides homes for bears, moose, squirrels, woodpeckers, deer, beavers, and other animals. Many feed on the nuts, berries, branches, and cones of such forests. Most coniferous forests stay green all year long.

Another kind of woodland is the *deciduous forest*, named from two Latin words that mean "to fall off." The broad leaves of deciduous trees fall off in autumn, and new leaves grow in the spring. Animals such as the cottontail rabbit, raccoon, chipmunk, opossum, and flying squirrel are able to survive in winter when the trees are bare and food is scarce. Some of them store food for the cold months, and some sleep away the winter in hibernation.

Creatures that live in *tropical rain forests* and *jungles* are used to the scorching heat and heavy rainfall there. In such forests in Africa, there are elephants, hippopotamuses, chimpanzees, and crocodiles. In rain forests of Asia, tigers, pythons, and gibbons are found. In Latin American rain forests, there are macaws, iguanas, toucans, jaguars, armadillos, and woolly monkeys.

Many animals live where there are few trees, or none at all. *Temperate grasslands* are flat, treeless plains in mild (temperate) climates. In the U.S.S.R. and Mongolia, such lands are called *steppes*. They are somewhat arid (dry) and have short grass. The Bactrian, or two-humped, camel is found in the steppes. In North America, the grasslands are called *prairies*. They have long grasses and are not as dry as the steppes. Pronghorns,

▼ *Cape buffalo were once common throughout Africa south of the Sahara, but hunting and disease have reduced their numbers in many places.*

prairie dogs, and coyotes are typical prairie beasts.

Savannas are grasslands found in tropical and subtropical regions. Some of the best-known savanna animals are those of Africa: lions, giraffes, vultures, leopards, zebras, rhinoceroses, and ostriches. In South America, the grassland animal population includes the maned wolf and the puma. Some unusual animals, such as the kangaroo, emu, and wombat, live in Australian savannas.

Many animals *migrate*, or move from one region to another, during certain seasons. Each year, North American robins, wild geese, and many songbirds escape the cold of winter by flying south to Florida or Mexico. In the Old World, numerous animals make their way from Scandinavian countries of Europe to winter in warmer Africa.

ALSO READ: ANIMAL HOMES, ECOLOGY, HIBERNATION, MARINE LIFE, MIGRATION, PLANT DISTRIBUTION, POLAR LIFE, POND LIFE.

ANIMAL FAMILIES Many animals work hard to raise their families. They give their young food, homes, and protection, and teach them how to take care of themselves. Other animals do not need to take care of their families at all.

Families are not important to most reptiles, amphibians, fish, and insects. Frogs, turtles, and most snakes lay eggs and leave them to hatch by themselves. The babies do not need parents because they know how to care for themselves as soon as they hatch. Such knowledge is called *instinct*. Most baby fish swim away by themselves after birth or after hatching. However, a few kinds of fish watch their eggs and even build nests. One fish, the stickleback, lives in both fresh and salt water. It builds an igloo-shaped nest on the ocean floor or in a stream. The female lays her eggs inside the nest, and the male guards them until the young hatch.

Most insects lay their eggs, and go away, never to return to them. But ants and bees build special nurseries for their young. Great numbers of worker ants or bees feed the young grubs, called *larvae*, until they become adults.

Families are important to birds and mammals because their young cannot survive alone. They need care and they must learn how to fend for themselves. Often both mother and father share the work. For example, a mother wolf seeks out a hidden spot, such as a cave, where she gives birth to her cubs. The father stands guard. Like all mammals, the mother feeds the tiny cubs with milk from her own body. The father helps to hunt food for them as they get older. Both parents teach the young how to hunt when the cubs are old enough.

▲ *Some animals need their mothers to get around, as well as to be fed. Here, a young monkey clings to its mother.*

◄ *A kangaroo carries its baby inside a pouch. The baby depends on its mother for food, transportation, and warmth. A baby kangaroo lives in its mother's pouch for weeks or even months before it begins to hop about.*

ANIMAL HOMES

▶ A young lamb can move around on its own, but it depends on its mother for food.

The strangest nest was probably one made by a sparrow in Switzerland. It was made entirely of watch springs.

Mothers alone care for the young of many other mammals. Fathers are not really needed. For example, deer do not eat meat, so the parents do not have to hunt food for the fawns. The mother deer, or doe, feeds them milk until they can eat plants.

Other mammal mothers have special problems with their young. Pouched mammals, or *marsupials*, such as kangaroos, are born so tiny and helpless that the young have to spend weeks or months in a pouch on the mother's abdomen. Even when a baby kangaroo can hop about on its own, it still returns to the pouch to escape danger.

Most birds build nests for their eggs. The parents often take turns sitting on the eggs to incubate them until the chicks hatch. The parents share the work of finding food to feed the chicks. In time, they coax the babies out for their first flying lesson.

But some birds do not build nests at all. The female emperor penguin lays a single egg on frozen snow. The male penguin immediately puts the egg on top of his feet where it is kept warm by his body. Groups of father penguins stay with the eggs for two months while the mothers swim out to sea to catch fish. When the eggs hatch, the mothers return. They begin months of feeding and protecting that allow the chicks to grow strong and independent.

ALSO READ: ANIMAL, ANIMAL HOMES, ANT, BEE, BIRD, CHILD CARE, MAMMAL, REPRODUCTION.

ANIMAL HOMES The beaver is one of the best-known animal homemakers. Beavers build a *lodge* of branches and mud on a riverbank, or even in the center of a pond. The entrance is always underwater, but the rooms inside are above the water. A lodge may house a single beaver family or be large enough for several families. Nearby, under the water, the beavers store a food supply of bark and other plants.

Like the beaver, other animals find or build homes that are specially suited for their way of life. Many birds make nests in high places, such as trees, chimneys, and barn roofs. Large birds, such as eagles and hawks, may build nests on mountain

eggs

▲ *Not all animals look after their babies. Tadpoles look after themselves from the moment they hatch.*

SOME ANIMAL FAMILIES

	Male Name	Female Name	Baby Name	Group Name
Kangaroo	Buck or Boomer	Doe or Flyer	Joey	Troop, Mob, or Herd
Cat	Tom	Puss	Kitten	Clowder
Dog	Dog	Bitch	Pup	Kennel, or Pack
Horse	Stallion	Mare	Foal (m or f)	Herd
			Colt (m)	
			Filly (f)	
Deer	Stag or Buck	Doe	Fawn	Herd
Hog	Boar	Sow	Piglet	Drove
Rabbit	Buck	Doe	Kit	Warren
Lion	Lion	Lioness	Cub	Pride
Chicken	Rooster or Cock	Hen	Chick	Flock
Fox	Fox	Vixen	Kit or Cub	Skulk
Swan	Cob	Pen	Cygnet	
Whale	Bull	Cow	Calf	Herd or School

◀ *Many spiders are expert web-spinners. This delicate trap of silk awaits flying insects. The spider pounces as soon as it senses prey struggling in the web.*

▼ *Harvest mice weave a ball-shaped nest of grasses. The nest hangs among the stalks of wheat.*

cliffs. Nests may be skillfully woven from twigs, weeds, mud, and other handy materials. A bird may even use pieces of old string, or bits of cloth or paper. Some birds prefer to nest on the ground. But birds to not live in nests all year round. They usually build them as a place to lay eggs in, and as a home for the chicks after they hatch. Between mating seasons, birds sleep any place that provides shelter.

The homes of social insects (insects that live together in groups) are also called nests. You may have seen a paper wasps' nest hanging from a tree. It looks like a round, gray paper bag. In fact, the nest is really made of paper. The wasps gather bits of dead wood and other tough plants, and chew them into a papery pulp. This pulp is then used to form the nest. Inside, there are usually many *cells*, or rooms, in which the queen lays eggs and the grubs, or *larvae*, develop.

The nests of bees are called *hives*. They are often dome-shaped or round, and made of chewed plants and wax. Wax is produced by the bees' own bodies. Honeybees also use wax to make *honeycombs* inside the hive, with cells for storing honey and for hatching eggs.

Prairie dogs and hamsters are also

▲ *Potter wasps mold mud and sand into hollow "pots" hanging from plants. Each pot contains an egg and food for the larva—in the form of a paralyzed grub or caterpillar.*

▲ *The ovenbird of South America uses mud, grass and leaves to build a nest rather like an old-fashioned oven.*

skillful builders of underground homes. Their homes are called *burrows*. Each prairie dog builds its own home, close to the homes of other prairie dogs. Each scoops up a small mound at the entrance to its burrow. This serves as a sunning place and as a watching post.

Some large mammals, such as wolves, bears, and mountain lions, may not build their own homes. Instead, they find a cave to live in. Such cave homes are known as *dens* or *lairs*. The females give birth to their young in the den. Bears use dens for their long winter sleep (hibernation). Certain kinds of bats live in caves, too.

Many other mammals have no home at all. Elephants, zebras, deer, and lions usually wander from place to place in groups or herds. Their needs are met by good feeding grounds, a water hole, and a temporary sleeping spot screened by trees or tall grass. But most animals, even if they do not build homes, occupy and defend a general area as their *territory*. An animal will stay within the limits of its territory (so long as it has enough food there), and will try to keep other animals away. A red squirrel, for example, may consider certain trees its "private property." Any creature that tries to move into the trees will get a loud scolding.

■ LEARN BY DOING

Find out about different animal homes, and make drawings of them. What is a muskrat's home like? How is an eagle's nest different from the nest of a robin? If you keep pet animals, such as rabbits or hamsters, think about how these animals' manmade homes may differ from their wild relatives' homes. Look around your home and neighborhood, and you'll be surprised to see how many wild creatures are at home there, too. ■

ALSO READ: ANIMAL DISTRIBUTION, ECOLOGY, PET.

ANIMAL INTELLIGENCE see INTELLIGENCE.

ANIMAL KINGDOM A great many different kinds of animals live on earth. Scientists realized long ago that they needed some way to group, or classify, animals. They figured out a simple way to group the many different animals by the structures of their bodies.

It would take a long time and much detail to describe completely a llama to someone who had never seen one. But if you said that the llama belongs to a family of long-necked, knobby-kneed mammals of the *artiodactyl* order, the person would already know, or could easily find out, a great deal about a llama.

Popular names for animals, such as "cat," "dog," or "llama" can describe very different animals in other countries of the world. So when a new animal is discovered, it is given a double personal scientific name by the discoverer. That name, the *genus* and *species* name, is recognized by scientists in every nation. Both genus and species are written in Latin. For example, the llama has the name *Lama glama*. No other animal has that same whole name. The guanaco, a relative of the llama, shares part of it. It is *Lama guanicoe*. Both animals belong to the same genus, *Lama*.

A species is a group of animals so alike that they can mate and produce young that are, in their turn, able to reproduce. Animals of two different species but in the same genus usually cannot mate and reproduce. A llama and a guanaco would not naturally reproduce.

Relating the Species A number of different genera (the plural of "genus") make up a *family*. The llama belongs to the camel family. Three different genera make up the camel family. Several different families make up an *order*. Llamas share the artiodactyl order with pigs, peccaries, hippopotamuses, deer, giraffes, and cattle. The members of all nine families in the order have three main things in common. First, they have an even number of toes on their feet. Second, their toes are covered with hoofs. Third, they have more than one chamber in their stomachs.

The order of even-toed hoofed animals shares an even larger group, called a *class*, with many other orders. Carnivores, bats, elephants, rodents, and even hoofed animals with an odd number of toes, make up some of the other orders in the class of animals called *mammals*. All mammals have body hair and feed their young with milk from the mothers' bodies. Most of them give birth to living young, but a few are so primitive that they lay eggs.

The animal kingdom is easily divided into animals with backbones (called *vertebrates*) and animals without backbones (called *invertebrates*). Mammals, birds, fish, reptiles, and amphibians are all vertebrates. But all of these animals are only part of one of the big groups into which the animal kingdom is divided. Such a big group is called a *phylum*. All vertebrates and a few other creatures belong to the *chordate* phylum. Chordates have a special elastic rod inside the body that acts as an internal skeleton. In the vertebrates, that rod has hardened into a backbone.

There are so many different kinds of invertebrates (more than 950,000 known species) that scientists put them in 25 to 35 phyla (the plural of *phylum*). Not all scientists agree on the exact number of invertebrate phyla. Some animals do not fit tidily into the main phyla. For example, the animals called *velvet worms* are not quite annelids (segmented worms such as the earthworm) and not quite arthropods (animals with jointed legs and hard coverings like the crabs and insects). The velvet worms, although there are only about 80 species of them, are usually put into a small phylum of their own.

A Kingdom of Animal Phyla   A description of the animal kingdom by phyla usually starts out with the very simplest animals, whose bodies are single cells, and leads up to the complex chordates. This kind of an arrangement may be very closely related to the way in which animals probably evolved on earth.

The first single-celled animals were not very different from the first single-celled plants. But over millions of years, the differences between most

▲ *The South American llama provides people with meat, milk, and wool. It carries loads as well.*

The giant tortoise lives longer than any other large animal. One lived for 177 years. But it is thought that some tiny bacteria can live many times as long.

The largest lobster is the American lobster. It can measure about 3 feet (1 m) in length and weigh up to 40 pounds (18 kg).

◄ *The guanaco of South America belongs to the same genus as the llama, but to a different species.*

THE ANIMAL KINGDOM

VERTEBRATES	**Chordates**	**15 Class Mammalia.** Examples of mammals are platypuses, echidnas, marsupials, moles, bats, seals, whales, cats, bears, horses, dogs (*shown*), and human beings.
		14 Class Aves. Examples of birds are geese (*shown*), sea birds, poultry, flightless birds, and birds of prey.
		13 Class Reptilia. Examples of reptiles are turtles, snakes (*shown*), lizards, and alligators.
		12 Class Amphibia. Examples of amphibians are frogs (*shown*), toads, salamanders, and caecilians.
		11 Class Pisces. There are three classes of fish: Agnatha (fish without jaws such as lampreys and hagfish); Chondricthyes (fish with skeletons of cartilage rather than bone, such as sharks and rays); and Osteichthyes (bony fish, such as the goldfish *shown*, cod, and salmon).
NON-VERTEBRATES	**Echinoderms**	**10 Phylum Echinodermata.** Examples of echinoderms are urchins, brittlestars, and starfish (*shown*).
	Arthropods	**9–8 Phylum Arthropoda.** Arthropods include insects, crustaceans, arachnids, centipedes, millipedes, and bristletails.
		9 Phylum Arthropoda, Class Insecta. Examples of insects are praying mantis (*shown*), butterflies, flies, beetles, bugs, and ants.
		8 Phylum Arthropoda. Class Crustacea. Examples of crustaceans are crayfish, lobsters, and crabs (*shown*).
	Mollusks	**7 Phylum Mollusca.** Example of mollusks include chitons, snails, clams (*shown*), oysters, squids, and octopuses.
	Annelids	**6 Phylum Annelida.** Examples of annelids are earthworms (*shown*), and leeches.
	Nematodes	**5 Phylum Nematoda.** Examples of nematodes (roundworms) are ascaris (*shown*) and hookworms.
	Flatworms	**4 Phylum Platyhelminthes.** Examples of flatworms include flukes, tapeworms, and planaria (such as Dugesia, *shown*).
	Coelenterates	**3 Phylum Coelenterata.** Examples of coelenterates are corals (*shown*), and jellyfish.
	Porifera	**2 Phylum Porifera.** All poriferans are sponges.
	Protozoa	**1 Phylum Protozoa.** Protozoans are the simplest animals. Examples are amoebas (*shown*), and Paramecia.

13

Snake

14

Goose

15

Dog

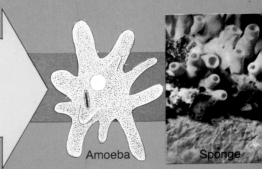
Amoeba   Sponge

1

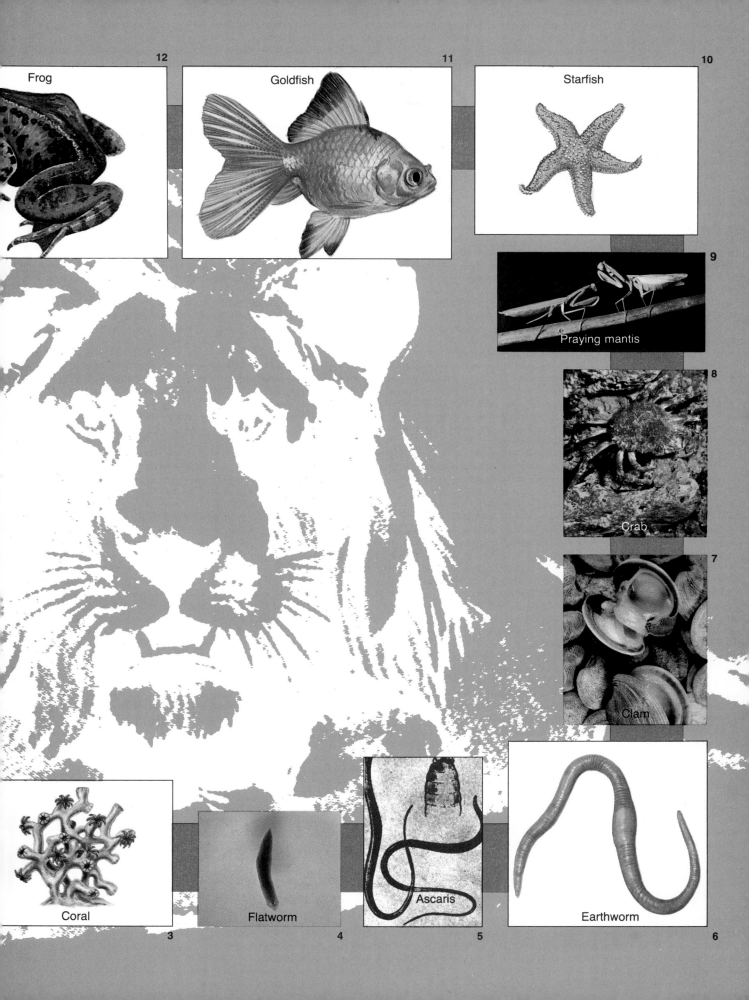

Frog 12

Goldfish 11

Starfish 10

Praying mantis 9

Crab 8

Clam 7

Earthworm 6

Coral 3

Flatworm 4

Ascaris 5

ANIMAL KINGDOM

It is difficult to calculate the speed of birds, especially in a dive. A peregrine falcon was timed at a speed of over 200 miles per hour (320 km/hr) diving over Germany. In level flight, a spinetailed swift has been timed at 106 miles per hour (171 km/hr). The fastest land animal over short distances is the cheetah, with a maximum speed of over 60 miles per hour (97 km/hr). The fastest racehorse travels at just over 43 miles per hour (69 km/hr). The slowest land mammal is the three-toed sloth. Its average speed on the ground is about 7 feet (2 m) a minute.

plants and animals became greater. There are still some single-celled creatures that are not neatly "plant" or "animal." They are called *protists*, which means "simplest organisms." Most scientists classify protists in a kingdom of their own, apart from the animal and plant kingdoms.

The simplest animals are called *protozoans*, meaning "first animals." A protozoan consists of only a single cell, but that single cell takes in air, food, and water, and gets rid of wastes—all the basic work of living done by more complex animals. The largest protozoans are little more than one-eighth of an inch (3 mm) long. Most can only be seen through a microscope. Amoebas are microscopic protozoans that live in water.

All phyla except Protozoa are made up of animals with many-celled bodies. They are called *metazoans*, which means "later animals." Some metazoans, such as sponges (phylum Porifera), are just masses of cells that are very much alike. Animals more complicated than the sponge developed gradually, over millions of years. Different groups of cells took on different tasks, and special systems of the body (such as the digestive system) developed. Animals that had heads and tails and shapes instead of just being globs of living matter

evolved, or developed.

So scientists group animals by the characteristics, or features, they have in common. Some of the characteristics cannot be easily seen by nonscientists. For example, there are many different kinds of wormlike animals. But they are put into several different phyla, depending on how complicated their digestive systems are, whether their bodies are smooth or segmented, and so on. One wormlike animal is even put into the most advanced phylum of all, the chordates.

The mysteries of the animal kingdom have not all been solved. Future scientists studying fossils, evolution, genetics, and anatomy may find some answers and even more questions.

For further information on:
Invertebrates, *see* AMOEBA, CENTIPEDE AND MILLIPEDE, COELENTERATE, COMB JELLY, CRUSTACEAN, EARTHWORM, ECHINODERM, INSECT, MOLLUSK, PROTOZOAN, ROTIFER, SPIDER, SPONGE.
Vertebrates, *see* AMPHIBIAN, BIRD, FISH, MAMMAL, REPTILE.
Science, *see* CELL; DARWIN, CHARLES; EVOLUTION; LINNAEUS, CAROLUS; PROTIST; REPRODUCTION; WALLACE, ALFRED RUSSEL.

Speeds are in miles per hour

Giant tortoise

Snail

Elephant

Giraffe

Zebra

Sea lion

0.03 0.05 25 32

ANIMAL MOVEMENT Many animals often move from one place to another. They search for food. They flee from danger. On land, animals walk, run, creep, leap, or glide. Many kinds of animals are also able to swim in water or fly through the air. Each kind of animal moves in the way that best helps it survive.

Many land animals use legs and feet for speed. The cheetah, a wild cat of Africa, is called the fastest animal on Earth—but only for a short distance. A cheetah can sprint for a short distance at 80 miles an hour (129 km/hr). Horses, deer, antelopes, and other speedy hoofed animals have long, powerful legs. The longer an animal's legs are, the farther it can go in one step. The ostrich cannot fly. But its legs are so strong that it can run faster than a horse.

■ LEARN BY DOING

Watch how different animals move. If you have a pet cat, notice how it walks, creeps, and runs. When a cat leaps down from a fence, which legs touch the ground first? Compare the way a cat walks with the way a dog walks. Watch horses and cows if you get the chance. Notice how these animals rise after lying down. What differences do you spot?

Make notes about the birds you see in your backyard or in the park. Do all birds run the same way on the ground? How about when they fly? Watch how an earthworm moves. Does it move in the same way as a snake moves? If you visit a marine aquarium, look at fish and then at whales and dolphins. How do these animals use their tails when swimming? ■

Insects have legs, too—six of them. Spiders have eight legs. Wormlike millipedes have up to 230 legs. Having so many legs can have many advantages, depending on the kind

▲ *Not until photography made possible stop-frame shots of running horses, in the 1800's, did people know for certain how a horse moved at speed.*

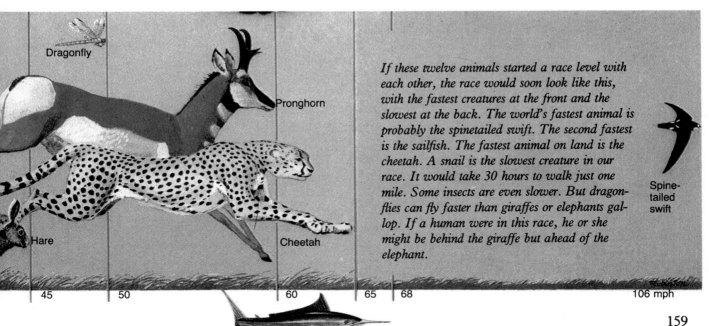

Dragonfly

Pronghorn

Hare

Cheetah

Spine-tailed swift

If these twelve animals started a race level with each other, the race would soon look like this, with the fastest creatures at the front and the slowest at the back. The world's fastest animal is probably the spinetailed swift. The second fastest is the sailfish. The fastest animal on land is the cheetah. A snail is the slowest creature in our race. It would take 30 hours to walk just one mile. Some insects are even slower. But dragonflies can fly faster than giraffes or elephants gallop. If a human were in this race, he or she might be behind the giraffe but ahead of the elephant.

45   50   60   65 68   106 mph

Sailfish

▶ *The sea turtle swims by using its flipperlike feet as if they are oars.*

▶ *The rabbit has particularly strong hind legs. It can jump well and run fast to escape its enemies.*

▲ *The mermaid was supposed to be half woman, half fish. Mermaids were said to lure sailors to their deaths. This unusual mermaid has* two *tails!*

of animal. These three kinds of animals all have jointed legs. This is a great help in moving quickly, easily, and powerfully.

Some animals do not depend entirely on legs to go places in a hurry. Many monkeys and gibbons use their arms to swing through trees. Frogs can jump from danger in one sudden, long-distance hop.

Not all land animals have legs for walking and running. A snail uses one muscle, called a *foot*, to pull itself slowly along. A snake has muscles that move its body in an S-shaped curve, pushing against rough spots on the ground. A fish can dart forward with a sideways flit of its tail fin. Like fish, whales and porpoises also use their tails for swimming power. But the tails of these sea mammals move up and down. Squids and octopuses sometimes jet-propel from place to place. When one of these animals wants to move, it sucks in water and then shoots out a jet through a tube in its body. This stream of water pushes the animal in the opposite direction.

Most birds move about by flying. A bird's bones are light and hollow. They are light to allow the bird to fly

more easily, but are strong enough to support the bird's body. Many adult insects, as well as bats (which are mammals) can also fly.

ALSO READ: ANIMAL, BONE, FLYING MAMMALS; articles on individual animals.

ANIMALS OF MYTH AND LEGEND
People told stories long ago of strange creatures and terrifying beasts. Some of the stories were myths, which often came from the religious beliefs of the people who told them. Other stories were legends, or popular stories that were handed down through the years. Legends and myths often told of animals that were not real. But people in earlier times believed they were. They did not know most of the scientific facts that people know today.

Some imaginary animals were part human. The *centaurs* of Greek mythology were half horse and half man. They were said to be wild and dangerous. They liked to fight and to destroy things. But one centaur, named Chiron, was kind and wise. Other Greek myths told of *satyrs*, gods of the woods. These mischievous creatures looked like men from the waist up, except for their pointed ears. From the waist down they looked like goats. *Mermaids* were lovely creatures with a woman's body and a fish's tail. They were seen by sailors at sea, sitting on rocks and singing beautifully while combing their long golden hair. Some, called *sirens*, were very dangerous. Sailors passing by could not resist the sirens' beauty. But when the sailors came near the island, their ships were wrecked on hidden rocks, and they drowned.

The *unicorn* is perhaps the most beautiful of legendary animals. It appeared in both Greek and Roman mythology. This animal was pure white. It looked like a small horse, but it had a tail like a lion's, and on its forehead was a single horn. Even in the Middle Ages, people in Europe thought that the unicorn really existed. Another fantastic animal was the *phoenix*, a bird with reddish-purple feathers. Egyptian and Greek myths say that the phoenix lived to be 500 years old. The bird would then set fire to itself and burn to death. But from its ashes a new phoenix would arise. The phoenix became a symbol of immortality (life that lasts forever).

Monsters   Many stories tell of imaginary creatures that are evil and frightening. The *dragon* was a fire-breathing serpent, or giant lizard. It appears in the myths and legends of many countries. In most stories, it was a horrible creature that often guarded a precious treasure. Only a brave hero could fight a dragon. In China, however, the dragon was re-

▲ *Greek legends tell of the centaur, which was half man and half horse. Most centaurs were wild and dangerous. But one, called Chiron, was a wise teacher.*

The Egyptians worshiped the cat. Killing a cat was a crime punishable by death. When a household cat died, its owner shaved off his eyebrows as a sign of grief.

◀ *Fierce griffins decorated palace walls in ancient Persia. The griffin was a royal guardian. It had a lion's body with an eagle's wings.*

garded as a god, not an evil monster.

The *chimera* and the *basilisk* are monsters of Greek myth. The chimera had the head of a lion, the body of a goat, and the tail of a serpent. It breathed fire, like the dragon. People sometimes use the word "chimera" to mean a foolish or wild idea. The basilisk was a very nasty beast. It was a birdlike serpent that could kill a person by breathing on him, or even just by looking at him.

The *werewolf* is another unpleasant legendary monster. A werewolf was human by day, but at night turned into a wolf and killed people. The werewolf appeared in Greek myth, as well as in legends of other countries.

Almost everyone has heard of *sea serpents*. These monsters appear in legends all over the world, and in all times. Such legends may have started when someone saw a real sea animal (such as a whale or giant squid) that was very strange and large. Some people claim that in Scotland today a giant serpentlike animal lurks in the depths of a great lake called Loch Ness. But scientists who have searched there have not yet located the monster. Another legend still believed today is that of the abominable snowman or yeti. This is said to be a hairy apelike beast that lives in the Himalaya Mountains in Asia.

Animals with Special Powers Not all legends tell of imaginary animals. Some tell of ordinary animals. But the legends show that people have thought that these ordinary animals had strange powers, or were special in some other way. The common house cat, for example, was worshiped as a god in ancient Egypt. The Hindus of India consider the cow a sacred animal. The Hindus will not allow cows to be killed, or even milked.

Animals play an important part in many American Indian myths. In a California Indian story, the Creator tried twice to make Earth (which the Indians thought was flat) stable and safe. But Earth kept wobbling. So the Creator sent a deer, an elk, and a coyote to stand at the northern end of Earth in order to steady it. This didn't work either, because the animals floated in the air. Finally, the Creator made them lie down. From that time on, the myth says, Earth was usually still. But Earth was disturbed by an earthquake if the animals moved. Another Indian tribe, the Iroquois (who lived in New York State), believed that Earth rested on the back of a very large turtle. In some Asian myths, the Earth rests

▼ *Dragons were sometimes good, sometimes evil. Here, Saint George, the patron saint of England, kills a dragon.*

► *The chimera was a fire-breathing monster from Greek legend. It had the head of a lion and the tail of a serpent, but was often shown with a goat's head emerging from its back.*

on the back of an elephant.

Babe, a giant blue ox, belonged to the legendary American giant, Paul Bunyan. Babe was born white, but he turned blue in the Winter of the Blue Snow. He was so heavy that his feet sank down to solid rock at every step. The legend says that Babe's footprints formed the many lakes in Minnesota.

People have feared, loved, and admired animals. All these feelings have come through in legends and myths. People have used the stories of fantastic creatures to explain strange happenings that they could not explain in any other way. Even when they know better, they may create legends about animals to express their feelings about life.

ALSO READ: ABOMINABLE SNOWMAN; BUNYAN, PAUL; FAIRY TALE; FOLKLORE; GODS AND GODDESSES; LEGEND; MYTHOLOGY.

ANIMAL TRACKS Animal tracks tell many stories. They are like written messages. They tell what kind of animal made them and in which direction it was going. They show whether it was hurrying—perhaps to escape an enemy—or taking its time. A person can learn to tell what an animal was doing by looking at its tracks.

A good time to track an animal—to follow its trail—is after a snowfall. A light snow, not deep enough for sledding, can be perfect for tracking. Animal footprints may also be found in mud, dust, and sand. Even tracks left by wet or muddy feet on concrete pavement can be helpful in learning about tracking. At the beach, tracks of sandpipers and other shoreline birds are commonly seen near the water.

You can learn important clues, which help in tracking wild animals, from the footprints of dogs and cats. You will notice a large heel pad and four smaller toe pads if you look very carefully at the paw prints of a dog or cat. Cat tracks are rounder and smaller than the tracks of most dogs. Cat tracks almost never show claw marks, because cats usually keep their claws drawn back when walking or running. Dog footprints do show claw marks. These differences between footprints are the same among wild members of the dog families. Wolf and coyote tracks look like the footprints of large dogs. Tracks of wildcats, lynxes, and mountain lions look much like those of a house cat, except that they are larger and some will show claw marks.

The different ways in which animals move are also shown by their tracks. For example, rabbits hop. They put their long hind feet in front of their front feet with each bound. A set of rabbit tracks shows two prints of roundish forefeet just behind the longer marks of the hind feet. The trail sometimes zigzags with sets of prints far apart, showing that the rabbit was escaping a pursuer.

The sharp, forked marks of bird tracks are easy to spot. If the bird's toes all show in the print, there are usually three in front and one in back. The footprints of ducks and other swimming birds show the outlines of webbing between the toes.

■ **LEARN BY DOING**

You can make copies, called *casts*, of animal tracks to collect and study. Find a clear print in the soil. Carefully remove loose leaves and twigs. Put a ring of heavy cardboard around the track. Into a bowl of water stir plaster of paris until it feels like a thick milkshake. Pour the plaster into the ring until the track is filled and the plaster touches the cardboard. When the plaster is completely dry, remove the cast. You have made a *negative*, or upside-down, cast. You can also preserve the track as it was in the ground. To make such a *positive* cast, put a layer of Vaseline on the negative cast. Put it back in the cardboard ring, and pour plaster of paris onto

In the Middle Ages people believed that the lizardlike salamander could pass through fire unharmed. Then, sometime later, a new material that could be spun and woven into fire-resistant fabric reached Europe. It was, people decided, salamander fur! Today we call it asbestos.

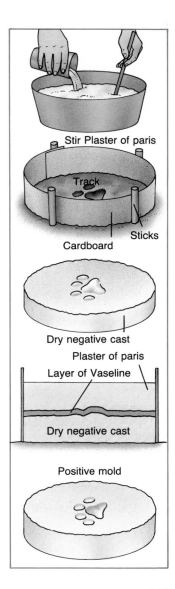

Stir Plaster of paris

Track

Sticks

Cardboard

Dry negative cast

Plaster of paris

Layer of Vaseline

Dry negative cast

Positive mold

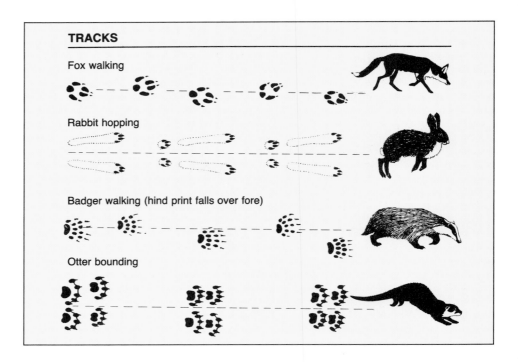

TRACKS

Fox walking

Rabbit hopping

Badger walking (hind print falls over fore)

Otter bounding

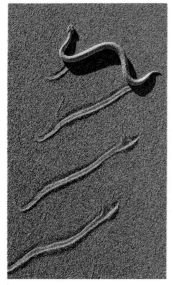

▲ *As the sidewinder moves, only two points of the snake's body touch the hot desert sand at any one time.*

the negative cast. When the plaster hardens, pull the two casts apart and wipe off the Vaseline. ■

Tracking is not always easy for a beginner. Few tracks are complete or perfect. Snow or dirt often falls on prints, covering or changing their shapes. The front feet of an animal may be different in size and shape from its back feet. But with practice and good detective work, animal tracking can become fascinating.

ALSO READ: ANIMAL MOVEMENT, HANDS AND FEET, NATURE STUDY.

ANIMAL VOICES Many animals make sounds. Dogs bark, frogs croak, roosters crow, birds sing, lions roar. Animals use their voices to send messages. Sometimes the message is to one of their own kind: "Here I am, come and be friends." Sometimes the message is less friendly, and is meant as a warning: "Here I am, keep away."

One of the most important uses for an animal's voice is to help it find a mate. Mating calls may only be made at certain times of the year. In spring, male frogs croak to attract female frogs. Birds sing to attract mates and also to warn off rivals. The squawking blue jay may be telling other birds, "Keep out of my tree!" Voices may be used to scare away enemies or to defend territory by warning others to stay outside. The loud roar of the male lion declares, "I'm the boss around here." Mother animals use their voices to call their young. For example, hens cluck to their chicks to keep them together.

Animals that live in groups, such as flocks or herds, often use voices to signal to each other. Flocks of wild geese honk. At sea whales and porpoises swim together in groups or schools and constantly give out whistles, grunts, and other calls to one another. Animals that hunt in packs, such as wolves and coyotes, yelp and howl to signal others to join in the hunt. As a rule, herd animals are noisier than animals that spend most of their lives on their own.

Most animal voices are produced by *vocal cords* in the throat. When air passes from the lungs and across the cords, the cords vibrate and produce sounds. Animal vocal cords are in a "voice box." In mammals, the voice

box is highly developed and is called a *larynx*. Birds have a simpler one, called a *syrinx*.

But not all animal sound signals are made by their vocal cords. Insects such as the cicada produce their mating calls by rubbing together parts of their bodies. Insects do not have proper voices, but can make a variety of buzzing and chirping noises in this way.

ALSO READ: SINGING, SOUND, SPEECH.

ANNAPOLIS see UNITED STATES SERVICE ACADEMIES.

ANNE (1665–1714) The last British monarch from the Stuart family was Queen Anne. She was the younger daughter of King James II, who was banished from Britain in 1688, during the Glorious Revolution. Anne's older sister Mary and Mary's husband William then took the throne as joint rulers, William III and Mary II. Anne became queen in 1702 after the deaths of Mary and William.

As a young princess, Anne had picked lively Sarah Churchill as her best friend. Sarah stood loyally by in the years when Anne and her hus-

band, Prince George of Denmark, quarreled with William and Mary. As queen, Anne rewarded her friend Sarah and Sarah's husband by naming him the Duke of Marlborough, and making him commander of the army. Marlborough was a brilliant soldier who had Anne's full support in his battles against the forces of the French king, Louis XIV.

A great event of Anne's reign was the union, in 1707, of England and Scotland under the name United Kingdom of Great Britain. Anne had 17 children, but all of them died. A German Protestant prince, George of Hanover, was chosen to be her heir.

Anne's reign is called the "Augustan Age," because leading writers and artists tried to reproduce the art of ancient Rome under Emperor Augustus.

ALSO READ: GEORGE, KINGS OF ENGLAND; WILLIAM AND MARY.

ANNIVERSARY An anniversary is a day celebrated each year in memory of a special event. Your birthday is the anniversary of the day on which you were born. In many places in the United States, people also celebrate the birthday of a famous person whom they admire, such as Abraham

Queen Anne is remembered in England and America by a tall, wildflower with a flat, white cluster of blossoms. It grows along the roadside, and is called Queen Anne's lace.

▲ *Queen Anne, last Stuart monarch of Britain.*

Wedding Anniversary	What Should The Gift Be Made Of?	Some Popular Gifts
First	Paper	Paper napkins
Second	Cotton	Cotton towels
Third	Leather	Leather wallet and key case
Fourth	Fruit, Flowers, Books	Four favorite books
Fifth	Wood	Wooden bookshelves
Tenth	Tin, Aluminum	Kitchenware
Fifteenth	Crystal, Glass	Crystal vase
Twentieth	China	Dinnerware
Twenty-fifth	Silver	Silver tea set
Thirtieth	Pearl	Pearl ring
Fiftieth	Gold	Gold watch
Sixtieth	Diamond	Diamond jewelry

There are more ants than any other social insect. At any time there are at least a quadrillion living ants on earth (1,000,000,000,000,000).

Lincoln (February 12) and Martin Luther King, Jr. (January 15).

Another kind of anniversary celebrates the "birth" of a state or a nation. Many U.S. states have celebrated their centennial—the 100th anniversary of the date on which they became states. One of the most popular national holidays in the United States is the Fourth of July, the anniversary of the country's birth as an independent nation. The United States celebrated its bicentennial—its 200th "birthday"—on July 4, 1976. This anniversary was so important, it was celebrated the whole year long.

Another common anniversary is the wedding anniversary, which marks the date when a couple was married. The three major wedding anniversaries, named for the type of gift that is often given, are the *silver* (after 25 years of marriage), the *golden* (after 50 years), and the *diamond* anniversary (after 60 years).

ALSO READ: HOLIDAY.

An ant can lift 50 times its own weight. This is about equal to your lifting a weight of two tons.

ANT The insects called ants live almost everywhere, from jungles to cities to mountains to deserts. Ants are "colonial" insects. They live in citylike *colonies*, made up of large numbers of insects that work together and help each other to survive. They fight wars with other colonies. You can usually spot an opening to an underground colony by the little mound of soil around it—the *anthill*. Other kinds of ants live in dead trees or even in houses.

There are several thousand different kinds of ants. All of them belong to the same order of insects as bees and wasps. All of these insects have *constricted* (pinched-in) abdomens and, when winged, have four clear, many-veined wings in two pairs, one smaller than the other.

The bodies of adult ants have three main parts—head, thorax, and abdomen. On the front of the head are two *antennae* (feelers). Ants use these for smelling, tasting, and touching. The thorax is the middle section of the body. The insect's six legs are attached to the thorax. Most kinds of male ants and most young queens have wings for a while, and these are attached to the thorax, too. The stomach and intestines are in the abdomen.

In each ant colony, there is usually just one *queen*, a small number of

▼ *Weaver ants at work. These ants skillfully fasten together the edges of leaves to make their nests.*

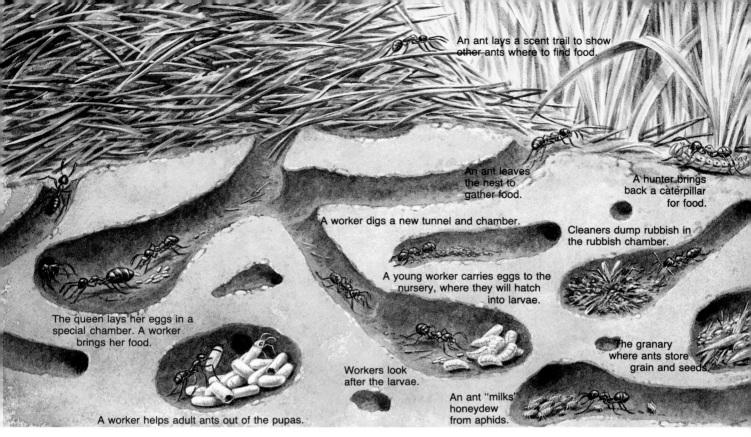

An ant lays a scent trail to show other ants where to find food.

An ant leaves the nest to gather food.

A hunter brings back a caterpillar for food.

A worker digs a new tunnel and chamber.

Cleaners dump rubbish in the rubbish chamber.

A young worker carries eggs to the nursery, where they will hatch into larvae.

The queen lays her eggs in a special chamber. A worker brings her food.

The granary where ants store grain and seeds.

Workers look after the larvae.

A worker helps adult ants out of the pupas.

An ant "milks" honeydew from aphids.

males, and a great many *workers*. Queens are usually larger than the other ants in the colony. They may live 20 years, and a single queen may lay millions of eggs. Male ants live only a few weeks. They die after they mate with a queen. Nearly all the ants in a colony are females called workers. The workers do not lay eggs. Instead they have several important jobs. Some take care of the queen. Others are "nurses," who care for the young. Others forage for food for the whole colony. And still others are soldiers and guards.

The queens and males usually fly from the nest to mate. The males then die. But the queens are ready to begin new colonies. After mating, a queen lays many eggs. Some eggs are fertilized and will become females. Others are not and will become males. The eggs hatch after several days or weeks into white, wormlike *larvae* (or grubs). "Nurse" ants feed and clean the larvae, and carry them if they must be moved. A few female larvae are fed special food. They will develop into new queens. The larvae become *pupas* after a few weeks or

months. Pupas appear inactive, or resting. The pupas of some kinds of ants are covered by a silklike cocoon. Many changes are going on during the pupa stage. These changes take place even though pupas cannot move about and do not have to be fed. Pupas finally emerge as full-sized adults.

The Ways Ants Live Different kinds of ants lead very different lives.

Leaf-cutters have jaws with sharp edges. The workers bite off pieces of leaves and flowers. They carry the pieces to their nest, where they make large piles. The queen plants bits of mushroom in these piles, and the mushroom "garden" that grows up provides food for the colony.

Harvester ants gather and store seeds, which they crush with their heavy jaws. If the seeds get wet, the harvesters carry them outside to dry and bring the seeds back into the nest at night.

Certain insects, such as aphids, are plant suckers. These insects produce a sticky, sweet fluid called *honeydew*, which some ants eat. The

▲ *Inside an ants' nest, each ant has its own special job as part of the colony. Some collect food, others look after the young. There are builders, cleaners, and soldiers. The most important ant in the nest is the queen.*

cow-keeping ants use these insects as "cows." They may "milk" the aphids for the honeydew by stroking them, or actually eat the insects. The ants do not, however, really "herd" or tend the aphids. *Honey ants* eat honeydew, too. But instead of milking aphids, they gather their supply from the leaves where plant-sucking insects drop their honeydew. Sometimes worker honey ants store the honey in their bodies. They often get so big and fat that they cannot move. Other ants in the colony get their honey from the mouths of these "living bottles."

Other ants, called *amazons*, are ferocious warriors. Their sharp, curved jaws are good for fighting but not for working. These ants keep slaves. They kidnap pupas from other nests. When the pupas develop, the captives spend all their adult lives working for the amazons.

Some other ferocious ants are the African *drivers* and their close relatives, the South American *army ants*. These ants do not build nests. They rest under logs or rocks for two or three weeks, while larvae are being hatched. Then the whole colony "marches" about looking for food. These ants will eat other insects,

young birds, and even small mammals that cannot get out of the way of their marching column.

Friend or Foe? Ants are a help to people most of the time. Ants, like earthworms, turn the soil and let air mix with it. Also ants pollinate some plants. Many ants eat other insects, some of which are harmful pests. By chewing up scraps of plant and animal stuff in their tunnels, ants and their grubs help enrich soil.

Ants do not always help people, however. Leaf-cutters ruin many plants. *Fire ants* have become a serious pest in the United States. They have a bite that can kill small animals and make people ill. They also build large mounds in fields that interfere with farm machinery. But overall, the damage that ants can do is not so important as the help that they give people.

■ LEARN BY DOING

Watch what happens when you disturb an ants' nest. See how the workers carry the eggs and larvae to safety. You can study the fascinating world of ants at leisure by carefully pushing a sheet of clear glass through the middle of the nest. Clear away the loose earth from the front of the glass, so that you can see into the nest. Behind the glass wall, the ants will go about their lives undisturbed. What happens when the new queens are ready to leave the nest? ■

ALSO READ: ANTEATER, INSECT, META-MORPHOSIS, TERRARIUM.

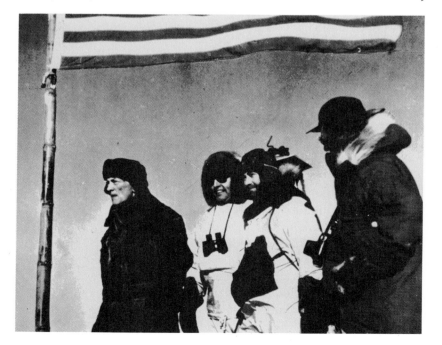

▼ *Richard E. Byrd (first at left) standing under the flag of the United States at the South Pole. Byrd stayed one winter (1933) alone near the Pole, making scientific observations.*

ANTARCTICA The southern continent of Antarctica is a great sheet of snow and ice. The snow and ice slope gently from a central *plateau* (a high, level area) around the South Pole toward the sea. Along the coasts of Antarctica, sharp mountains rise up from the snow. Huge masses of ice called *glaciers* slide between the

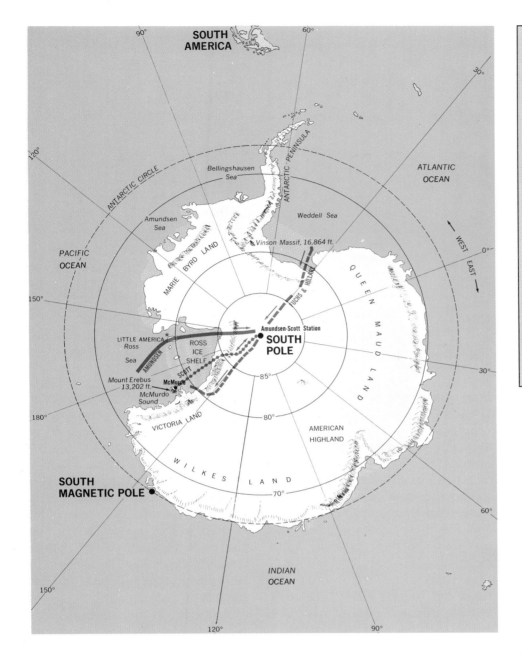

SOUTH AMERICA

90°
60°
30°
0°
120°
ANTARCTIC CIRCLE
Bellingshausen Sea
ATLANTIC OCEAN
Amundsen Sea
Weddell Sea
MARIE BYRD LAND
ANTARCTIC PENINSULA
Vinson Massif, 16,864 ft.
PACIFIC OCEAN
WEST EAST
QUEEN MAUD LAND
FUCHS & HILLARY
150°
Amundsen-Scott Station
SOUTH POLE
LITTLE AMERICA
Ross
ROSS ICE SHELF
85°
30°
AMUNDSEN
SCOTT
Mount Erebus 13,202 ft.
McMurdo
Ross Sea
McMurdo Sound
VICTORIA LAND
80°
AMERICAN HIGHLAND
180°
SOUTH MAGNETIC POLE
WILKES LAND
70°
60°
150°
INDIAN OCEAN
120°
90°

ANTARCTICA
Area About 5,500,000 square miles (14,244,000 sq. km).
Coastline About 13,800 miles (22,208 km) long.
Highest point Mount Vinson Massif, 16,864 feet (5140 m).
Lowest point Sea level.
Population No permanent residents. Many scientists, and explorers visit the continent to study the area.
Resources Large coal deposits in east Antarctica. Probably other minerals. Fish and plankton in the surrounding seas.

mountain ridges toward the sea. At the sea's edge, tremendous icebergs break off the glacier and float away. They are often enormous. One iceberg is said to have been the size of Delaware.

The Land and Snow Beneath the snow and ice of Antarctica lies land. Snow piles deeper and deeper on top of the land and hardens into ice. In some places, it is 3 miles (4.8 km) deep. Near this great frozen land mass is a chain of smaller islands. One of the islands has an active volcano,

Mount Erebus. The islands and the land mass are joined into one continent by a thick blanket of ice.

Antarctica has nine-tenths of all the world's ice. If all this ice melted, the level of the world's oceans would rise 250 feet (76 m) Most cities along the coast would be drowned. In New York harbor, water would almost cover the Statue of Liberty. But Antarctica stays well below freezing all year in most places. It is the coldest place on Earth. Inland, winter temperature falls to −100°F (−73°C).

Antarctica is actually a desert.

▼ *A researcher in Antarctica measures the movement of a glacier.*

ANTARCTICA

▶ *Antarctica is covered by ice, but peaks called* munataks *stick up in places at the coast. The ice breaks off to form huge flat-topped icebergs.*

Fossil animals and plants have been found in Antarctica. This shows that the continent has not always been a cold and apparently lifeless place. Some of the largest coal and oil deposits in the world are believed to lie buried beneath the vast Antarctic ice cap.

Antarctic fish do not freeze solid when the sea freezes. This is because their blood contains a natural "antifreeze"—a complex chemical substance that stops the formation of ice crystals in the fishes' bodies.

Most people think of a desert as a very hot and dry place. Antarctica is certainly not hot, but it is very dry. All its water is frozen. Only about 5 inches (130 mm) of snow fall there each year, which is less moisture than some of the world's hot, sandy deserts receive each year. The little snow that does fall on Antarctica piles up over the years, because not much of it melts.

Plant and Animal Life Like other deserts, Antarctica does not have much plant life. Only a few kinds of trees and simple plants, such as mosses, lichens, and algae, can grow there. The climate is so harsh, and food so scarce, that people have not settled in Antarctica. But along the coasts of the continent there are many birds, fish, and mammals.

The Antarctic waters are rich in *plankton* and *krill*, tiny sea creatures that provide food for fish and whales. Thousands of whales and millions of seals swim in Antarctic seas. Six kinds of seals are found. The fur seal, the smallest, has long been hunted for its silky fur. The vicious leopard seal, which can grow up to 12 feet (3.6 m)

long, has powerful jaws and sharp teeth. It eats fish and penguins. The elephant seal is the largest. It can weigh as much as 4 tons (3.6 metric tons). Other kinds of seals are the Ross, Weddell, and crabeater.

The blue whale is the largest animal that has ever lived. It may weigh as much as 150 tons (136 metric tons) and be 95 feet (30 m) long. Smaller whales include the bottlenose, the humpback, the sperm, and the finback.

A number of birds live in Antarctica. Petrels, terns, cape pigeons, and skuas fly over the water and ice. The Arctic tern has been called the long-distance champion flier. Each year it migrates between the northernmost islands of the Arctic (the region around the North Pole) and the shores of Antarctica—a distance of about 11,000 miles (17,700 km)

Penguins are the best-known of Antarctic birds. They cannot fly, but their flipperlike wings make them strong swimmers. Penguins eat fish. The large emperor penguin looks as if it were dressed in a tuxedo for a formal dinner. The Adélie penguin, which is smaller than the emperor, lives in very large colonies along the coast and seems to enjoy getting in the way of scientists working in Antarctica.

Exploring the Icy Continent
Antarctica was the last continent to be discovered. Explorers had long wondered if a southern polar continent existed. In 1772, Captain James Cook, a British explorer, started a three-year voyage of exploration in which he sailed completely around Antarctica but never sighted the continent's mainland.

In 1820, Americans hunting for fur seals were the first to sight the "forgotten continent." But Antarctica was not proved to be a continent until 1840, when the American naval lieutenant Charles Wilkes completed a voyage along the coast. Then other explorers came to Antarctica, traveling inland on foot.

The "race to the South Pole" between a Norwegian explorer, Roald Amundsen, and a British explorer, Robert F. Scott, took place in 1911. Amundsen and his men reached the Pole first and returned safely. Scott and his men got there a month later. But they died from cold and lack of supplies on the return trip.

A later explorer, Sir Hubert Wilkins of Australia was the first to fly over Antarctica in 1928. Admiral Richard E. Byrd of the U.S. Navy flew over the South Pole in 1929. (Byrd was also the first man to fly over the North Pole.) In 1929, Byrd set up a permanent base camp called *Little America* on the Ross Ice Shelf. Byrd led five expeditions to Antarctica.

Sir Vivian Fuchs led a British Commonwealth expedition that was the first to cross Antarctica from coast to coast, in 1958. The explorers made the 2,158-mile (3,472-km) trip with big snow tractors in 99 days.

Today, a number of nations share a scientific interest in Antarctica. An agreement made in 1959 and now signed by 32 nations says that none will claim territory for itself or use it for military purposes. There is now a permanent manned base at the South Pole. Scientists go to Antarctica to measure glaciers, study weather, and learn more about its history and rocks, its plants and animals. Antarctica has been called "the world's greatest scientific laboratory."

ALSO READ: AMUNDSEN, ROALD; ARCTIC; BYRD, RICHARD E.; CONTINENT; COOK, CAPTAIN JAMES; EARTH; EXPLORATION; GLACIER; PENGUIN; SCOTT, ROBERT F.; SEALS AND SEA LIONS; WHALES AND WHALING.

▲ *Antarctica's wildlife must be hardy to survive. The emperor penguin carries its chick on its feet, sheltered in a warm fold of skin.*

MAJOR EVENTS IN ANTARCTICA

1772	Captain James Cook sailed around Antarctica, but sighted no land.
1838–40	Lieutenant Charles Wilkes proved Antarctica was a continent by sailing along its coast.
1911	Roald Amundsen first reached the South Pole, winning the race against Robert F. Scott.
1928	Sir Hubert Wilkins became the first man to fly over Antarctica.
1947	Admiral Richard E. Byrd led Operation Highjump, the largest Antarctica expedition ever organized up to that time.
1956	The United States Navy started to establish permanent bases.
1957–58	Scientists participating in the International Geophysical Year studied all aspects of Antarctica.
1958	Sir Vivian Fuchs first crossed Antarctica coast to coast.
1966	Nicholas Clinch climbed Mount Vinson Massif and other peaks.
1967	Peter J. Barrett found fossils proving that Antarctica once had a warmer climate.
1985	Twenty-four nations met in Antarctica itself to discuss the Antarctic Treaty, and how best to use Antarctica for the world's benefits.

ANTARES Ancient sailors used the brightest stars to navigate their ships. One of the brightest stars in the sky is Antares. It is located in the constellation Scorpius, which can be seen in the south during summer evenings. This star has a diameter of about 300 million miles (483 million km), which is larger than the Earth's orbit around the sun.

Antares is a red star, about 330 light years from Earth. Someone looking at Scorpius hundreds of millions of years ago would have seen Antares as a white star. It was then only a few times larger than the sun. Since that time it has swollen into a red "supergiant," shining about 4,000 times as brightly as the sun. Antares is also a "double star." Powerful telescopes show a much fainter hot, blue companion star nearby, and the two stars take hundreds of years to revolve around each other.

ANTEATER Several different animals are called anteaters because they eat mainly ants or termites ("white ants"). Many anteaters have heads and mouths adapted for gathering their food. For example, the aardvark, sometimes called the *cape anteater*, has a narrow head and a sticky tongue. The echidna or *spiny anteater* of Australia does, too. The pangolins of Africa and Asia, which look like armadillos, are also known as *scaly anteaters*. They look like insect-eating pine cones, especially when they curl up inside their shields of overlapping scales.

Mainly, however, the name *anteater* is used for three mammals that live in the hot, humid forests of Central and South America. Like armadillos and sloths, these mammals lack some or all of the usual mammal teeth. The order of mammals to which armadillos, sloths, and anteaters belong is called Edentata, which means "toothless." Anteaters have no teeth at all. They have a tubelike mouth containing a long tongue. They have strong, curved claws for breaking open termite nests. Female anteaters usually give birth to only one baby a year. It rides on the mother's back for several weeks after it is born.

The largest of the three American anteaters is the *giant anteater*. It lives on the ground. Its body is about three feet (90 cm) long, with a bushy tail that adds another three feet. It has a gray coat. On its shoulders are black marks edged in white. The body color blends with sunlight and shadow, helping to hide the animal from its enemies. The giant anteater wanders alone, searching for food, stopping only to curl up and sleep. It is sometimes called an antbear.

The *tamandua*, or *collared anteater*, is only half as big as the giant anteater. The tamandua lives in trees, where it can cling to branches with its

▲ *The dwarf anteater can use its tail as an extra arm to grip onto a tree branch.*

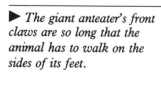

▶ *The giant anteater's front claws are so long that the animal has to walk on the sides of its feet.*

strong, almost hairless tail. Its fur is yellow-brown with a darker vest and collar.

The smallest anteater is the *dwarf anteater*, also called the *silky* or *two-toed* anteater. It is about the size of a large squirrel. Unlike the stiff fur of other anteaters, its golden hair is very soft and silky. The animal often lives in silk-cotton trees, which bear silk-like fruit pods that match the anteater's fur coat. The silky anteater can grip the tree with its tail and defend itself with its two long claws.

ALSO READ: AARDVARK, ARMADILLO, MAMMAL, SLOTH, SPINY ANTEATER.

ANTELOPE Antelopes are grazing animals known for their speed, their graceful, high leaps, and their beautiful, curiously shaped horns. Their closest relatives are the quiet and not-very-swift cattle. Both antelopes and cattle are *ungulates* (hoofed animals). Antelopes, like cattle, have an even number of hoofed toes, and horns instead of antlers. They eat plants, and they chew cuds.

▼ *The saiga antelope lives on the wide steppes (plains) of central Asia.*

Antelopes are fast-moving, nervous animals. They need to be alert, for they are a favorite prey of meat-eating animals such as lions and tigers. Antelopes must be prepared to eat their food and run. Later, in safety, the animals chew balls (or *cuds*) of the plant food they swallowed earlier. Animals that chew cuds are called *ruminants*.

Deer are ruminants, too. But deer have antlers made of bone that are shed and replaced every year. Antelopes have horns that grow only once in a lifetime. Both male and female antelopes usually have horns. Baby antelopes are able to run with the herd soon after birth.

There are almost 100 kinds of antelopes, differing mainly in size and kinds of horns. The tiny *royal* antelope, which looks like a rodent, lives in forested western Africa. Its small horns barely show above the hair on its head. The *sable* is a large horselike antelope of southern and eastern Africa. Its magnificent horns can be up to 4 feet (1.2 m) long and curve backward in an arc. The desert-living *common oryx* has short, perfectly straight horns. The *blackbuck* of India has ringed horns that look like giant corkscrews. The *impala* of the African savanna (grassy plains) has horns

The largest antelope is the eland. It is about 6 feet (1.8 m) high at the shoulder and weighs about a ton. Its spiral horns grow to a length of 4 feet (1.2 m).

▼ *The American pronghorn is not related to true antelopes.*

▶ *Three female blackbucks leap gracefully through the night. Blackbucks are medium-sized antelopes commonly found in India.*

The word "antelope" comes from the Greek *antholopos*, meaning brightness-of-eye. Antelopes' eyes are very large and bulging. This allows the animals to look around without moving their heads.

shaped like a lyre, a small musical instrument similar to a harp.

Antelopes also differ in their living conditions. Many kinds live in deserts, far from water. The *addax* lives in the Sahara Desert of northern Africa. It has large hoofs that keep it from sinking in sand. The little water it gets comes from plant roots which it digs out of the sand.

The graceful *gazelles* live on open plains in Africa and Asia. They are small- to medium-sized animals with lyre-shaped horns. A herd of gazelles fleeing from danger is a wonderful sight. A *springbok* gazelle can leap 10 feet high (3 m) or cover 20 feet (6 m) in one jump while running at a speed of 65 miles an hour (105 km/hr).

The large and very heavy *giant eland* of forests and plains in western Africa looks more like an ox than an antelope. But even it can leap over high bushes in one movement. The *brindled gnu* or *wildebeest* is also like an ox, but it gallops quickly when pursued by lions. The *duiker* lives in thick underbrush in African forests. It is no bigger than a large rabbit. The *reedbuck* lives in marshes, where it wades for plants to eat.

The *pronghorn*, an animal that North Americans call an "antelope" actually belongs in a different family from real antelopes. It has horns that are shed every year. The male's horns are 12 inches (30 cm) long and have small prongs curving toward the front near the top.

The pronghorn is America's fastest mammal and also one of its rarest. When a pronghorn in the herd sees danger, it raises the white patch of hair on its rump as a warning signal to the others. Pronghorns can run 60 miles an hour (97 km/hr) for a short time. Coyotes hunt pronghorns by taking turns to chase them, until the pronghorns are exhausted.

ALSO READ: DEER, HOOFED ANIMALS, HORNS AND ANTLERS, MAMMAL.

ANTHONY, SUSAN B. see WOMEN'S RIGHTS.

ANTHROPOLOGY Human history seems short compared to that of rocks, oceans, fish, other mammals, birds, and other features of the Earth.

But there are still many puzzles about human beings and how they developed the way they did. People who try to solve these secrets are called *anthropologists*.

Anthropos is the ancient Greek word for mankind. So "anthropology" means "the study of mankind." It is a fairly recent science, which began in the 19th century.

Most anthropologists concentrate on one of the four main branches of anthropology—physical anthropology, archeology, cultural anthropology, and linguistics. The *physical anthropologist* wants to know how and when people began to do things that no other animal can do. Physical anthropologists often study ancient human bones that have been found deep in the ground. By comparing these bones with the bones of modern humans, they can learn how the human body has changed over hundreds of thousands of years. Physical anthropologists also try to understand why there are different groups of humans—why, for example, do some people have brown skin, while others have white or yellow skin? They compare the groups to see how they are alike as well as how they are different.

The *archeologist* is interested in learning how the people of ancient civilizations lived. What did they wear? What kind of food did they eat? What did they believe? What were their customs? Archeologists dig in the earth, looking for tools, clothing, or pottery that might give a clue about the lives of the people who once used them. One of the most important archeological discoveries has been the Valley of the Kings, near Cairo, Egypt. This place was a cemetery for the *pharaohs* (kings) of Egypt more than 3,000 years ago. From the more than 60 tombs discovered so far, archeologists have found out many things about how the ancient Egyptians lived and what they thought.

The *cultural anthropologist* is concerned with the everyday life of peo-

ple living today all over the world. These scientists study the customs, arts, beliefs, governments, and economy of a people. A cultural anthropologist can also be called an *ethnologist*, which means "one who studies people."

Ethnology in the past was the study of people in isolated areas of the world, far from civilization. Ethnologists offered explanations for cultures, languages, and races in terms of historical migrations. They found it easier to study small groups, such as the aborigines of Australia and New Guinea, who still lived much like their ancestors did thousands of years ago.

Today, ethnologists or cultural anthropologists are comparing past and present cultures to learn how racial and ethnic groups have changed. They are particularly interested in how people from ancient cultures adapt to modern life, with its complex machines and scientific inventions. To study these groups, anthropologists may live with them.

▲ *Richard Leakey, the anthropologist, compares the cast of a skull 2½ million years old (top) with that of a million-year-old* Australopithecus.

▼ *Anthropologists often study the funeral and burial customs of ancient peoples. This tall stone is a* menhir, *a funeral monument built in the Bronze Age.*

▲ *Anthropologists are interested in our earliest ancestors. This is* Australopithecus, *a manlike ape that lived about 1 to 4 million years ago in Africa. Skulls and bones of these creatures have been discovered.*

Some anthropologists make a special study of *linguistics*, the science of language. By studying the language of a people, the linguist can learn much about their knowledge and beliefs. Many linguists are particularly interested in languages that are spoken but have never been written down, such as those of certain American Indian and African tribes. Other linguists study "dead" languages—those that are no longer spoken, such as Old Hebrew, or written, such as ancient Egyptian hieroglyphics.

Applied anthropology uses what anthropologists have discovered to help solve modern problems. Anthropology can shed new light on how our bodies grow, what foods are good for us, and why some people commit crimes.

Anthropologists have done much to help people of different cultures understand one another. One of the most famous American anthropologists was Margaret Mead (1901–1978).

ALSO READ: ABORIGINE, ARCHEOLOGY, CULTURE, CUSTOMS, HUMAN BEINGS, SOCIOLOGY.

ANTIBIOTIC Antibiotics are substances that help the body fight against bacteria and other germs. Doctors use antibiotics to treat diseases caused by bacteria. When someone is sick with such a disease, a course of injections or capsules of an antibiotic can control the disease. Millions of lives have been saved since antibiotics were first used in 1941. Most antibiotics are produced naturally by plants so small they can be seen only under a microscope. Most antibiotics that doctors use are produced by *molds*. Molds are a type of *fungus*, a simple plant that cannot make its own food.

Today, many different antibiotics are used to treat infections. *Penicillin*, the first antibiotic used in medicine, is

▲ *Thousands of millions of bacterial cells, covering this drum like a white paste, are needed to make enzymes in the manufacture of penicillin antibiotics.*

still the best known. It was discovered accidentally in 1928 by Alexander Fleming, a British scientist. He noticed that a certain blue-green mold stopped the growth of bacteria. He tried unsuccessfully for more than ten years to separate from the mold the chemicals that stopped bacterial growth. He finally succeeded in 1940, with the aid of two other scientists, Howard Florey and Ernst Chain. They named the new drug "penicillin" after *Penicillium notatum*, the mold that produces it.

The first person treated with penicillin was a policeman dying of blood poisoning. Florey injected penicillin into the policeman's veins, and the man began to get better. But there was not enough penicillin in the shot to stop completely the growth of the bacteria poisoning his blood. He became ill again, but Florey had no more penicillin. So the policeman died.

Although the patient died, Florey had proved that bacterial infections could be successfully treated with penicillin. All Florey needed was a large quantity of penicillin. He went

▼ *A mold of* penicillium. *Fleming, Florey, and Chain helped turn this natural growth into an antibiotic that saved thousands of lives.*

to the United States and there persuaded drug companies to grow *penicillium* mold. The companies produced large amounts of penicillin during World War II in time to save the lives of thousands of people who might otherwise have died from infected wounds.

Scientists have found many more useful antibiotics, such as *tetracycline*. This drug is used to fight whooping cough, infections in the stomach and intestines, pneumonia, Rocky Mountain spotted fever, typhus, and many other diseases that once killed many people every year.

ALSO READ: BACTERIA; DISEASE; DRUGS AND DRUG ABUSE; FLEMING, SIR ALEXANDER; FUNGUS; MEDICINE.

ANTIDOTE   see FIRST AID, POISON.

ANTIGEN AND ANTIBODY   If an army breaks into a fort, the soldiers inside fight to push the enemy out. The body defends itself against disease in a similar way. *Antigens* are parts of foreign invaders—any disease-causing agents, such as bacteria, snake poisons, or viruses, or even harmless substances like pollen. The body makes weapons, or *antibodies*, to fight the invading antigens.

A person's body makes large amounts of antibody when he or she has an infection. Antibodies are made in special places, such as in the glands under the arm or in the tonsils in the throat. These glands become large and active when they must produce great amounts of antibodies. So people get swollen throats and necks or lumps in the armpits when they are sick with certain diseases.

Antibodies travel through the bloodstream to the infected parts of the body. They are chemical agents that inhibit the growth and spread of bacteria or viruses. Often, in a few days, the antibodies overcome the vi-

rus, and the person feels better. (Sometimes, though, the sick person will need medicine to help, too.) If a person is "attacked" by the measles virus, the antibodies "remember," and if the virus attacks the body again, the antibodies can often remove the invader so quickly that the person will not even feel ill. If a person has had measles, he or she will probably not get it again—they have *immunity* to it. The body becomes immune to most common diseases. Vaccination can also produce immunity.

ALSO READ: BLOOD, DISEASE, IMMUNITY.

ANTIGUA   see WEST INDIES.

ANTILLES   see WEST INDIES.

ANTIMATTER   Scientists keep finding more and more, and stranger and stranger tiny particles inside the atom. To add to the complication, they have also found out that all these particles have twin particles that are exactly opposite to them in every way. These particles are called *antiparticles* and they make up *antimatter*.

The antiparticles to the electrons that spin around the center of atoms are called *positrons*. Electrons have a negative electrical charge; positrons have an exactly equal and opposite positive charge.

Antimatter does not exist naturally on Earth. If it did it would meet ordinary matter and there would be a tremendous explosion. Whenever an antiparticle meets an ordinary particle the two destroy each other completely and there is a burst of radiation. However, scientists can produce short-lived antiparticles in their big *particle accelerators*.

ALSO READ: ATOM, MATTER.

The use of molds as antibiotics is not new. The Chinese, 2,500 years ago, used the molding curd of soybeans to treat boils and other infections.

Some people think that there may be some galaxies far away from us in the universe that are made entirely of antimatter.

▲ *Many people collect Greek and Roman antiques. Here is a Greek vase they called an amphora. The Greeks painted scenes on their vases, showing heroes and gods.*

ANTIQUE The skillful artists of the ancient world created beautiful objects, such as sculpture and jewelry. Sculptors often worked with materials that they knew would last, such as bronze, marble, or other stone. Jewelers worked with gold, silver, and precious gems. Many such works of art were collected by people who valued beautiful objects. Greece and Rome produced many valuable works of art. Long after Greece and Rome were no longer great powers in the world, some of these treasures were preserved.

During the Renaissance period in Europe, wealthy people started to collect objects from the ancient world. They called these objects *antiques*. Antiques were valued because they were a record of the past, as well as being beautiful old things.

The word "antique" slowly grew in meaning to include any very old object that is valued as a work of art or that reminds people of an earlier time. Antiques are often costly works of art such as painting or sculpture, but they can also be practical items such as furniture, lamps, household utensils, tools, musical instruments, and fine carpets. Some collectors think that an object must be at least 100 years old to be an antique. But people collect younger objects that have a nostalgic or rarity value—such as old cars, old clothes, and old records.

Antique collecting is popular all over the world today. Some people buy antiques so they can sell them later for higher prices. Some buy them to show their wealth and good taste. Some collect old objects, such as coins, as a hobby. And some just like the look and feel of beautiful old things.

■ LEARN BY DOING

What is the oldest thing in your home? Look around and find out. Almost every family has something old—a gold watch from grandfather, an old Bible, a letter from long ago. What was life like when these old things were made? ■

▶ *Cradles are the first beds for many babies. This antique cradle is made out of wood. It has flowers carved into the sides. Some old cradles are passed down from parent to child for many years.*

▶ *It is fun to collect only one kind of antique, just as you may collect shells or stamps. Some people collect old watches like this French one. See how it has covers to protect the face and back.*

Antiques come from almost everywhere in the world. Much antique furniture comes from Europe, America, and the Orient (eastern Asia). European and American furniture is often grouped by the general style of the furniture built during a period of years, such as Regency (early 19th-century English) or American Colonial. Furniture may also be grouped by the area from which it comes or by the name of the designer—for example, Chippendale or Duncan Phyfe. A piece of Chinese furniture takes the name of the dynasty (a long line of rulers who belonged to the same family) during whose rule it was made.

It does not take expert knowledge or great wealth to become an antique collector. A person may decide to collect old spoons, or perhaps miniature lamps that were once used as night lights, or old books and maps, or even toys. People can learn as they collect antiques. Libraries, museums, shopkeepers, and antique shows help collectors learn to know different kinds of antiques.

In a way, everyone lives with antiques—the antiques of the future. A hundred years from now, a favorite toy, chair or picture—even this encyclopedia—may be an antique treasure in someone's home or in a museum collection.

ALSO READ: COLLECTING.

ANTISEPTIC Cut fingers or scraped knees should be washed with soap and water to make sure the injury is clean. The soap acts as an *antiseptic* to prevent infection in the break in the skin. The word "antiseptic" comes from two Greek words that mean "against poison."

Antiseptics, such as soap and other chemicals, kill bacteria (germs) or stop their growth. Hot steam and ultraviolet light are also good at killing bacteria. Bacteria cause swelling,

fever, pain, or sickness if they get into the bloodstream. Skin usually keeps them out. An antiseptic stops the growth of harmful bacteria while broken skin is growing back together again.

ALSO READ: BACTERIA, DISEASE.

ANTONY, MARK see CAESAR, JULIUS; CLEOPATRA.

APACHE INDIANS Bands of the Indians now called Apaches probably wandered to the U.S. Southwest from Canada along the eastern flanks of the Rockies about A.D. 1000. The tribe's name was given to them by a neighboring tribe, the Zuni. The Zuni word *Apachu* means "enemy." The Apaches earned their name for they often raided villages of other tribes when food was scarce. In better times, the men hunted buffalo and other game. The women picked wild plants and grew squash and corn. Apache families lived in *wickiups*, houses built of branches. Women owned the wickiups, and both men and women spoke at the tribal meetings.

The Apaches were good hunters and warriors. White men and other Indians respected and feared their

▲ *George Washington lived in a house in Virginia named Mount Vernon. You can still go there today and see many antiques. They did not have a stove in those days, so they heated the food and the kitchen with a fireplace. How many antiques can you find in the old kitchen?*

▲ *Even toys can be antiques. This toy is over 1,000 years old. It looks like a strange buffalo with wheels. When you were younger you probably had similar toys which you pulled with a string.*

▲ *An Apache woman and child.*

warlike ways. Apache leaders, such as Cochise and Geronimo of the Chiricahua band, terrified white settlers. The Apaches fought to preserve their way of life and to protect their lands for almost 40 years after New Mexico became United States territory. They resisted the whites until 1886 when the U.S. army captured Geronimo.

About 12,000 Apaches live in Arizona and New Mexico today. Many of these Native Americans live on reservations. Some raise cattle, cut timber, and work in industry.

ALSO READ: ATHABASCAN; COCHISE; GERONIMO; INDIANS, AMERICAN; INDIAN WARS.

APARTMENT   see HOUSE.

▲ *The chimpanzee is the ape most like human beings in some of its behavior.*

▼ *The gorilla is the most powerful of the apes. But it is a shy and gentle plant eater.*

APE   When Americans were getting ready to send men into space, they wanted to be sure that it would be safe. So first they decided to send up an animal as much like a man as possible. They chose a chimpanzee. A chimpanzee is an ape—one of the most highly developed animals.

Apes—together with lemurs, monkeys, and human beings—are members of the order of mammals called *Primates*. The four main kinds of apes are the chimpanzee, the gorilla, the orangutan, and the gibbon. They live in hot, humid forests of Africa and Asia, and feed mainly on fruits, leaves, and nuts, although some apes steal birds' eggs and others may catch small animals for food.

The body of an ape is like the human body in many ways. For this reason, apes are sometimes called *anthropoid* ("humanlike") apes. Apes have no tails, unlike most monkeys. They have muscles, nerves, and organs (such as the appendix) that are similar to a human's. Their bones are also like a human's, but their arms are longer and their legs shorter. The lower end of the ape's backbone is straight, not curved. This makes it possible for the ape to walk standing up straight, although most apes prefer to walk on all fours. Another important trait that apes share with humans (and other primates) is the *opposable* thumb. It can move in opposition to, or against, the other fingers, so the thumbed hand can grasp food and other objects readily. But unlike humans, the ape has opposable thumbs on its feet as well as on its hands.

An ape's skull is thicker than a human's, and its brain is not so large or complicated. Next to the human being, the ape is one of the most intelligent of all animals. Possibly only the dolphin, a sea mammal, is as smart. Apes are quick to learn, and they can even be taught to use tools. Some scientists claim that apes can learn a simple form of human language.

The *chimpanzee*, of central West Africa, is the brightest of all the anthropoid apes—and probably the most popular among humans. Chimpanzees live in bands, or groups, and have a complex social organization. Young chimpanzees are especially playful, and love to show off skills they have learned. Adult "chimps," particularly males, become less playful. A full-grown chimp weighs as much as a grown man but is only about 5 feet (1.5 m) tall. Its face and hands are usually black or pink, and its fur is long and black.

The biggest and strongest of the apes is the *gorilla*, also found in West Africa. The full-grown male gorilla stands up to 6 feet (1.8 m) tall and weighs about 400 pounds (180 kg). Because he is so heavy, the adult male has to stay on the ground when his family climbs into a tree nest to sleep. Gorillas have broad shoulders, powerful arms, and strong jaws. When a male gorilla is in danger, he often tries to scare away his enemy with loud noises, but he usually does not stand up and beat his chest with his fists. Gorillas look fierce but they are really very shy. Of all the apes, only the gorilla is a strict vegetarian (vegetable-eater) that never eats another animal.

The *orangutan* is found only in Borneo and Sumatra. Its name means "old man of the woods." It spends almost all its time in trees. The orangutan has a reddish brown coat,

It has been proved that chimpanzees can distinguish as many color variations as human beings.

The average adult chimp is about as intelligent as a human child before the child learns to take its first steps.

▼ *The orangutan is an ape that spends almost all its time in forest trees.*

▲ *Gibbons are the smallest apes. Their very long arms are adapted for swinging through the trees.*

stands about 4 feet (1.2 m) tall, and weighs about 200 pounds (90 kg).

The smallest of the apes is the *gibbon*. It is much smaller than the other three, which are known as "great apes." The gibbon weighs from 12 to 20 pounds (5–9 kg), and stands from 17 to 39 inches (43–99 cm) tall. It spends much of its time in the trees. It has very long arms and can move very fast, swinging hand-over-hand from branch to branch. On the ground, the gibbon walks upright, balancing its arms over its head, like a small child learning to walk. Seven kinds of gibbon live in Southeast Asia and Indonesia. Many have white, woolly hair when they are born, but the color changes as they grow. Some gibbons, including the lar gibbon, keep some of their white coloring, usually around the face and on the hands and feet. The siamang gibbon, which is the largest gibbon, is known for its loud cries. It cries are amplified through a throat sac.

Because of their close similarities to humans, apes are among the most fascinating of animals. They have been used extensively in scientific and medical research, and are mostly protected in the wild.

ALSO READ: MAMMAL, MONKEY.

APOLLO   see MYTHOLOGY.

APOLLO SPACE PROGRAM see ASTRONAUT, MOON, SPACE TRAVEL.

APOSTLES From his many followers, or disciples, Jesus Christ chose 12 people to carry on his work of teaching and healing. These were the Apostles, a name that comes from the Greek word for messenger, or somebody who is "sent out." After the death of Jesus, it was the responsibility of the Apostles to spread the Gospel, or "good news" of Christ.

The 12 Apostles were: Simon Peter and Andrew, his brother; James and John, the sons of Zebedee; Matthew, or Levi, the tax collector; Philip; Bartholomew, or Nathanael; Thomas, also called Didymus ("Doubting" Thomas); James, son of Alphaeus (called "the Less" to distinguish him from the other James); Thaddeus, believed to be the same person as Judas, or Jude; Simon "the Zealot"; and Judas Iscariot, the traitor. After the death of Judas Iscariot, his place among the 12 was taken by Matthias. Of the Apostles, Peter, James, and John were especially close to Jesus.

Other followers of Jesus are sometimes called Apostles, including James, writer of the Epistle, as well as Paul and Barnabas. Paul called himself the Apostle to the Gentiles (that is, non-Jews). Like the 12, he claimed to know the truth of the risen Christ and to have been commissioned through him to follow in his work. All the Apostles of Jesus were sent out on at least two trial journeys to preach and heal. The story of their activities after the death of Jesus is told in the fifth book of the New Testament of the Bible, which is called the Acts of the Apostles. It was written in Greek and, it is said, by Luke, the author of the third Gospel. The first part of Acts tells how the early church was set up among the Jews in Judea; the second part describes the journeys of St. Paul and the founding of the Christian church among the Gentiles.

ALSO READ: BIBLE, JESUS CHRIST.

APPALACHIAN MOUNTAINS

The Appalachians are a long chain of mountains reaching from eastern Canada to central Alabama. These mountains are smooth and low compared with the Rocky Mountains, because the Appalachians are much older and more eroded, or worn. The highest point in the chain is Mount Mitchell, North Carolina, which is 6,684 feet (2,037 m) above sea level. (See the map with the article on NORTH AMERICA.)

The Appalachians are known by various names in different places. Canada has the Notre Dame Mountains. New England has the Green Mountains and White Mountains. The Adirondacks lie in New York, and the Alleghenies run from Pennsylvania to Virginia. Virginians and North Carolinians call one range the Blue Ridge Mountains. In Kentucky are the Cumberland Mountains, and along the North Carolina–Tennessee border stand the Great Smoky Mountains. A footpath, the *Appalachian Trail*, runs along the Appalachian ridges for about 2,000 miles (3,220 km), from Maine to Georgia. It has camping sites and hiking paths.

Many rivers begin in the Appalachians. The Potomac, Delaware, Savannah, and other rivers flow eastward and empty into the Atlantic Ocean. The Allegheny and Monongahela rivers meet at Pittsburgh, Pennsylvania, to form the Ohio River, which flows westward into the Mississippi. These rivers cut gaps through the mountains. Thousands of early

In the many pictures that have been painted of the apostles, they are often shown with a special sign or symbol that can be recognized. St. Peter, for example, carries keys, St. Andrew is seen with a cross like an X, St. John has an eagle, and St. Matthew a winged lion.

▼ *Leonardo da Vinci painted this picture of the Last Supper. It shows Jesus with his closest followers, who became apostles and spread the message of Christianity after Jesus' crucifixion.*

▲ *The forest-covered Appalachian Mountains, worn smooth by time, were crossed by explorers and hunters heading West. This is a view of Grayson Highlands State Park.*

▲ *Johnny Appleseed, the gentle frontiersman who loved to plant apple seeds.*

settlers traveled through these gaps to the West. Daniel Boone led hundreds of pioneers along the Wilderness Road—from Virginia through the Cumberland Gap to Kentucky.

ALSO READ: BOONE, DANIEL; CAMPING; EROSION; MOUNTAIN; NORTH AMERICA; RIVER; WILDERNESS ROAD.

APPENDIX   see DIGESTION.

APPLESEED, JOHNNY (1775–1847)   Stories from pioneer days tell of a man who loved apple trees, who spent his life planting apple seeds and giving away little apple trees. His name was John Chapman, but he became famous as "Johnny Appleseed."

He first got apple seeds from a cider mill in Pennsylvania. He planted them in a garden along the Ohio River. When the seeds had sprouted into seedlings, he gave away the trees to people who were heading west, to plant near their new homes.

Johnny Appleseed became well known on the frontier. He wandered through the wilderness carrying a Bible and leaving pages of it for the pioneers. Indians thought anyone who looked and acted like Johnny was protected by the Great Spirit. He once summoned U.S. troops to Mansfield, Ohio, preventing an Indian attack during the War of 1812.

Some people thought he was crazy to spend his life planting trees he would not live to see. But for many years after his death, thousands of apple trees from Pennsylvania west through Ohio, Indiana, and Illinois bore fruit.

ALSO READ: PIONEER LIFE.

APPRENTICE An apprentice is a beginner who agrees to work for a skilled craftsman in order to learn an art or trade. During the Middle Ages, parents or lords of manors often arranged for a boy to learn a trade from an experienced craftsman called a *master*. The master would usually *apprentice* the boy for seven years. The master taught his craft and gave the boy food and shelter—but no pay. Then the apprentice became a *journeyman*. He was free to travel and earn wages; he might, after much more experience, even become a master himself.

In the Middle Ages no one could set up in a trade without first learning it as an apprentice. A master had power to do whatever he liked with his apprentices. Sometimes apprentices were ill-treated. But if they had a good master, they were usually well cared for.

The apprentice system still exists today, with some differences. The Bureau of Apprenticeship and Training, within the United States Department of Labor, works with unions, vocational schools, and other groups to set up apprenticeship and training programs. Today, nearly 100 trades offer apprenticeships in about 300 special jobs in the U.S. For example, apprentices can learn to become bricklayers, airplane mechanics, electrical workers, and barbers. Many apprentices graduate from high school before beginning training. Some apprenticeship programs include classes in technical schools. Apprentices are often paid as they learn. As in olden times, today's apprentices may later become masters of their trades. They may finally end up running their own businesses.

ALSO READ: CAREER, EDUCATION.

▼ *Apprentices in the Middle Ages were examined in their crafts by a guild master, as this 15th-century illustration shows. On the left is a stone carver, on the right a carpenter.*

APRIL "Sweet April showers do bring May flowers." This little poem was written hundreds of years ago. The month of April often does have many rain showers. April is the fourth month of the year and has 30 days. The sweet pea is the flower for April, and the diamond is the birthstone of the month. The word "April" comes from the Latin word *Aprilis*, which means "to open."

April is usually the beginning of spring in the temperate zone of the Northern Hemisphere. In the far north, the weather is still icy cold. In the Southern Hemisphere, April is the beginning of autumn, a harvest time for grain, not a sowing time as on northern farms.

The first day of April is a fun day— April Fool's Day. The custom of playing silly, harmless jokes on other people on April 1 began in France in

▲ *The sweet pea is the flower of April.*

DATES OF SPECIAL EVENTS IN APRIL

1 ● April Fool's Day.

2 ● Hans Christian Andersen, Danish writer of children's stories, was born (1805).
● First movie theater opened in Los Angeles, California (1902).

3 ● Pony Express began over a route of 1,900 miles (3,057 km) from St. Joseph, Missouri, to Sacramento, California (1860).
● Jesse James, the famous outlaw, was killed (1882).

4 ● President William Henry Harrison died one month after inauguration (1841), and
● John Tyler became tenth President of the United States.

5 ● Booker T. Washington, black U.S. educator, born (1856).

6 ● Robert Peary reached the North Pole (1909).
● United States declared war on Germany (1917).

8 ● Flower Festival in Japan honors the birthday of Buddha.

9 ● General Robert E. Lee surrendered to General Ulysses S. Grant at Appomattox Court House, ending the Civil War (1865).

11 ● Jackie Robinson became the first black to play in major league baseball when he joined the Brooklyn Dodgers (1947).

12 ● Civil War began at Charleston, South Carolina, when Confederate troops opened fire on the U.S. Army at Fort Sumter (1861).
● President Franklin D. Roosevelt died (1945), and
● Harry S. Truman became thirty-third President of the United States.
● Yuri Gagarin became the first man in space when he orbited the Earth (1961).

13 ● President Thomas Jefferson was born (1743).

14 ● Pan American Day celebrates friendship and cooperation among the nations of America.
● George Washington elected first President (1789).
● President Abraham Lincoln shot by John Wilkes Booth (1865).

15 ● President Lincoln died (1865), and
● Andrew Johnson became seventeenth President of the United States.
● Ship *Titanic* sank after hitting an iceberg in the North Atlantic (1912).
● Chesapeake Bay Bridge-Tunnel—the world's longest bridge-tunnel—was opened (1964).

18 ● Paul Revere, William Dawes, and Dr. Samuel Prescott made their famous midnight ride to warn the patriots that the British were coming (1775).
● San Francisco destroyed by earthquake and fire (1906).

19 ● Battle of Lexington, Massachusetts, began the American Revolution (1775).

21 ● Spanish-American War started (1898).

22 ● Oklahoma Territory opened up to settlers (1889).

23 ● Saint George's Day, the patron saint of England.
● Traditional birth date of William Shakespeare, the famous playwright (1564).
● First public showing of a movie took place in New York City (1896).

25 ● First shots of Mexican War were fired (1846).

26 ● British colonists made first permanent settlement in America at Jamestown (1607).

27 ● President Ulysses S. Grant was born (1822).

28 ● President James Monroe was born (1758).

30 ● First public television broadcast took place from Empire State Building in New York (1939).

the 1500's. The Christian celebrations of Easter and Palm Sunday and the Jewish festival of Passover usually come in April.

ALSO READ: CALENDAR, EASTER, HOLIDAY, MONTH, PASSOVER, SEASON, SPRING.

AQUARIUM An aquarium is a tiny reproduction of a water environment. It can be a beautiful, interesting, and convenient way to study plants and animals that live in water, if it is properly made and cared for.

A successful aquarium must have both animals and plants. Plants give off oxygen and provide food for animals. Fish breathe in oxygen from plants and breathe out carbon dioxide. Carbonic acid—which plants need—is made when carbon dioxide mixes with water. This is a *balanced* aquarium.

The best kind of aquarium is a rectangular glass-sided tank. Most beginners start with 10-gallon (38-liter) tanks.

Making an Aquarium The three main kinds of aquariums are *freshwater*, *tropical freshwater*, and *marine* (saltwater). Each of them needs special care, but some rules are the same for all. Here are some basic steps to follow if you want to set up an aquarium.

(1) Wash sand or gravel and spread a layer about 2 inches (5 cm) thick on the bottom of the tank.

(2) Fill the tank with water. Carefully press some plants into the gravel, tall ones in back, short ones in front. If you buy your fish from a pet store, ask for some good plants to go with them. *Hint*—put a clean piece of paper on the sand or gravel before you pour the water in. This prevents the water from stirring up the sand. Remove the paper—it will float on the top of the water—after the tank is filled.

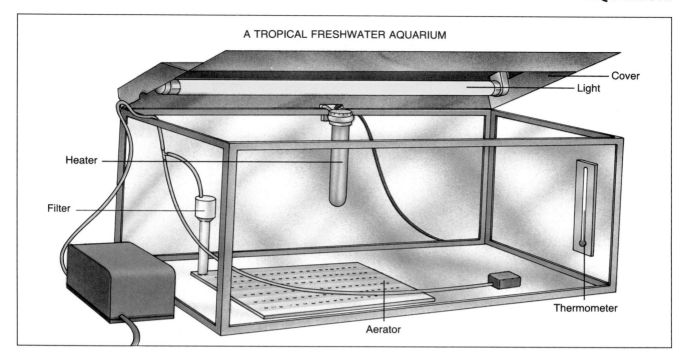

A TROPICAL FRESHWATER AQUARIUM

Cover

Light

Heater

Filter

Thermometer

Aerator

(3) Be sure that the water temperature is close to that of your fish's natural home. Pet stores sell a special thermometer that hangs inside the tank. Tropical fish need warm water—75° to 80° F (24° to 27°C). You should buy a heater that fits into the tank and controls the water temperature.

(4) Most aquariums need an *aerator*, a little pump that bubbles air through the water and provides extra oxygen for the fish. Pet stores sell aerators which often include filter systems that keep the water clear and clean.

(5) Place the tank where it gets plenty of light, but not too much direct sunlight. Direct sun can kill plants and cause tiny green algae to grow and spoil the water. You can buy a small electric light that hangs from the top of the tank.

(6) Always try to buy young fish in pairs. Young fish are usually cheaper and healthier than older ones.

(7) Let your aquarium water stand overnight before putting in the fish. Carefully transfer your fish from the plastic bag or container into your tank. Never touch tropical fish with your hands.

(8) Cover the tank with a piece of glass after the fish are inside to keep them from jumping out, to prevent dirt from falling in, and to slow down evaporation. But make sure air can get in by raising the glass just a little. Always keep the tank very clean. Remove dead fish or rotted plants right away, before they start a disease. Catfish and snails are useful aquarium inhabitants, because they eat scraps. Include a few of these *scavengers*. But snails reproduce very rapidly. Remove young snails, or soon there will be so many that they will destroy the balance of living things. Learn to recognize the tiny, clear ball-shaped snail eggs, so that you can remove the whole cluster of eggs at once. Pet

▼ *An aquarium should be designed with care. Rocks disguise the corners, while placing tall plants behind bushy ones gives an illusion of distance. The side view picture shows how the gravel is sloped upward, from front to back.*

AQUARIUM

▶ *Many species of fish will live happily in a home aquarium. These are Congo Tetra, from Africa.*

The ancient Romans dug huge ponds which they stocked with rare and valued fish. But it was the ancient Chinese who first started keeping fish indoors. They bred carp to produce the beautifully colored and strangely shaped goldfish we see today.

stores also sell tools for cleaning the tank's floor.

(9) Try not to crowd your fish. A good rule is to allow 2 inches (5 cm) of fish length for 1 gallon (3.8 liters) of water. A 10-gallon (38-liter) tank can safely hold ten 2-inch (5-cm) fish, twenty 1-inch (2.5 cm) fish, or one 20-inch (50-cm) fish.

(10) Read more about the kind of aquarium you want, or get advice from a hobbyist or a pet-store owner.

Freshwater Aquariums The simplest aquarium is a freshwater one, in which you can keep small fish from local lakes, rivers, or ponds. Carp, catfish, small bass, crappie, and bluegill are some of the favorites. The fish can be captured in a jar or net and kept in the same water in which they normally live. If you use tap water, let it stand for a few days before you put the fish in. Otherwise, harmful gases in the water can kill the fish.

Carp and catfish eat almost anything, dead or alive. Small pieces of liver or beef are good foods for them. Bass, crappie, and bluegill eat live food, such as earthworms. Never put in more food than the fish will eat in a short time.

A freshwater tropical aquarium is the most popular kind. Watching the colorful fish and the delicate plants in a tropical aquarium is like watching a miniature scene of tropical underwater life. Never use pond or river water in a tropical aquarium, because the tiny organisms that live in pond water will kill the fish. Use tap water, but let it stand for two or three days before you put the fish in. You can use rocks for decoration, but do not use gypsum, alabaster, limestone, or metallic ores. These rocks are poisonous to fish. Safe rocks are quartz, sandstone, petrified wood, and shale.

Many kinds of beautiful fish can be kept in tropical aquariums. Guppies are good fish for beginning hobbyists. Baby guppies are born alive, not hatched from eggs. Guppies can stand some changes in temperature, and they do not get sick as easily as many other kinds of tropical fish. Give all your fish room to swim by keeping one area of the tank free of plants and rocks.

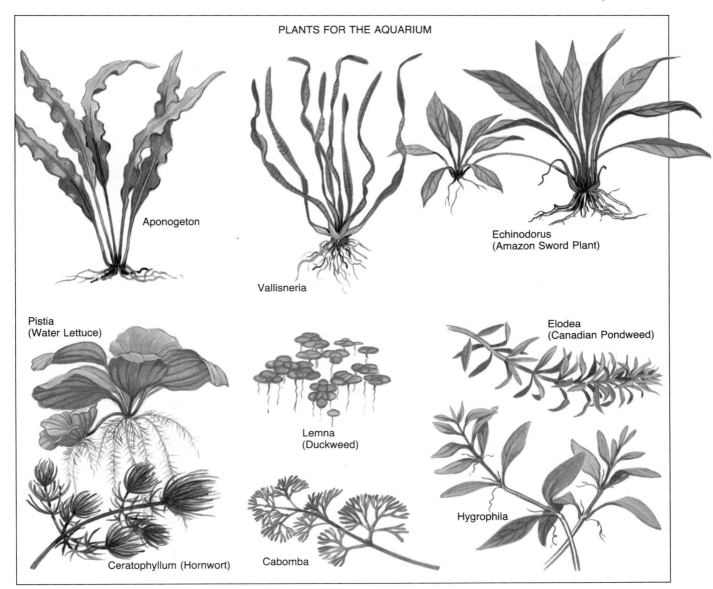

PLANTS FOR THE AQUARIUM

Aponogeton

Vallisneria

Echinodorus
(Amazon Sword Plant)

Pistia
(Water Lettuce)

Lemna
(Duckweed)

Elodea
(Canadian Pondweed)

Hygrophila

Ceratophyllum (Hornwort)

Cabomba

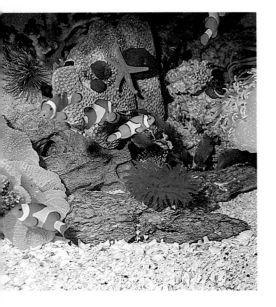

You can buy tropical fish food in most pet stores. Tropical fish also like tiny tubifex worms (available in pet stores) and mosquito larvae. A plastic feeding ring is handy, because it floats on the surface and keeps the food from spreading all over. The food drops to the bottom in one place and is easy to clean up. Any food that the fish do not eat in five minutes should be removed, so that it does not rot in the tank.

◄ *A marine aquarium has fewer plants than a freshwater tank. But living coral makes a good home for the fish, sea anemones, and other sea creatures.*

The world's largest aquarium is the John G. Shedd Aquarium in Chicago, Illinois. There are over 300 different kinds of fish on display.

189

The vast area of Saudi Arabia has no permanent rivers or lakes. Most of the country is desert, so there are only about 13 people to the square mile (5 per square km).

More than 600,000 Muslims from 60 nations visit Muhammad's birthplace, Mecca, every year. Because Mecca is so sacred, only Muslims are allowed to enter the city's gates.

Marine Aquariums It is possible to set up marine aquariums without living near an ocean, but they are hard to prepare and maintain. Special all-glass aquariums and artificial sea water are available in pet stores. Water will evaporate from the aquarium, and what is left will become too salty. So artificial sea water must be added from time to time to keep the correct salt level. Sea anemones, sea horses, barnacles, coral, mussels, and small crabs are good animals for marine aquariums. Sea lettuce and other small ocean plants belong in the aquarium, too. Sea horses and crabs eat small pieces of meat. Sea anemones, coral, mussels, and barnacles eat tiny animals and plants that live in ocean water.

■ **LEARN BY DOING**

It is fun to study the water life in your aquarium. Do some kinds of fish hide in plants or near the bottom while others dart everywhere? Are there differences between baby fish that hatch from eggs and those that are live-born? Do catfish or other scavengers have different habits from other kinds of fish? An aquarium can give you answers to these questions, as well as many others about the habits and life cycles of water animals and plants. ■

ALSO READ: ANIMAL, ANIMAL HOMES, ECOLOGY, FISH, HOBBY, OXYGEN, PLANT, SNAILS AND SLUGS, TERRARIUM, TROPICAL FISH.

AQUINAS, SAINT THOMAS (about 1225–1274) As a young student, Thomas Aquinas was called "dumb ox" by his classmates because he never talked much in class. Yet he grew up to become one of the great teachers, writers, and philosophers of the Middle Ages.

He was born near Aquino, in Italy. At 19, he joined the Dominican order of friars, preachers who supported themselves by begging. This angered his wealthy family. While he was traveling with the friars, his brothers carried him off by force and imprisoned him in the family castle for a year. Aquinas did not give up his dream of serving God. In 1245, he began to study in Paris under Albertus Magnus, a famous religious scholar. He followed Magnus to Germany, but returned to Paris to teach theology.

His writings on Christian philosophy and teaching have been important in the Roman Catholic church for hundreds of years. Many of his writings were gathered into a large three-part book called *Summa Theologica*. His influence on Christian thought has been powerful. Thomas Aquinas was declared a saint in 1323. He was proclaimed a doctor of the church by Pope Pius V in 1567. He is the patron saint of Catholic schools.

ALSO READ: PHILOSOPHY.

ARABIA Arabia is a large boot-shaped peninsula between the Red Sea and the Persian (or Arabian) Gulf, forming the southwest corner of Asia. It occupies slightly more than a million square miles (2.6 million sq. km), about one-third the size of the United States. The peninsula is divided between eight countries. Much of the area is barren desert where few people live. The weather is extremely hot during the summer months—dry in the interior and humid on the coasts. On many parts of the peninsula, summer temperatures often reach 120° F (49°C) in the shade. The southern edge of Arabia may receive around 20 inches (500 mm) of rain a year. But in the interior desert years may pass with no rain at all.

Spring and autumn are pleasant seasons. As in many desert regions, days are sunny and warm, and nights—with bright stars and brilliant moonlight—are cool. Winter (December through February) tempera-

▲ *Thomas Aquinas, a great Christian philosopher.*

tures drop below freezing in central and northern Arabia. But snow usually falls only on the highest areas. In late summer, when the days are burning hot, desert nomads and city dwellers all watch for the constellation Carina to appear in the sky. Its appearance is said to mean that the worst part of summer is over. Other constellations mark the other changes of seasons.

In the past, Arabia was best known as a crossroads between the cultures of East and West. It was a center of trade and of learning. The Arab system of numbers (Arabic numerals), on which arithmetic is based, was taken by Western traders to Europe in the 12th century. One of the world's great religions, Islam, originated in Arabia in the 7th century. Islam now has more than 550 million followers worldwide. Arabia today is known for its vast deposits of oil, the source of billions of dollars of income to the economy each year.

Arabian History Sumerian traders crisscrossed Arabia 5,000 or more years ago. They were followed by others, the Babylonians, Assyrians, and Persians. All of these traders left parts of their civilizations behind in Arabia. Phoenician sailors dropped anchor at bustling Arabian seaports 1,000 years before Christ. And the ancient Romans called the southwest coast of the peninsula *Arabia Felix*, Fertile Arabia. The region was a trade center for frankincense, myrrh, ivory, silk, spices, copper, gold, and jewels.

The prophet Muhammad was born in the city of Mecca (now in Saudi Arabia) in the year A.D. 570. He converted many Arabs, especially the poor and the slaves, to his new faith, Islam, and then set out to carry his

▶ *Arabia is the birthplace of Islam, the religion founded by Muhammad. Muslims are forbidden to show Muhammad's face, so in this painting he is veiled.*

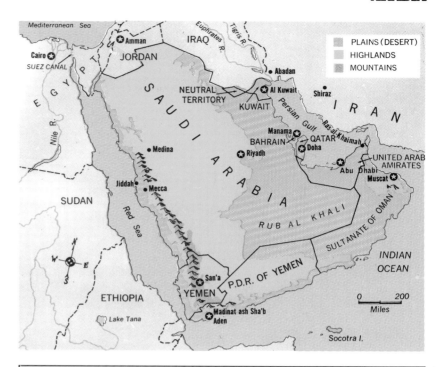

ARABIA

	Area (sq. mi.)	Area (sq. km)	Capital	Currency	Products	Population
Bahrain	240	622	Manama	Dinar	Oil	480,000
Kuwait	6,880	17,818	Kuwait	Dinar	Oil, chemicals	1,970,000
Oman	82,036	212,457	Muscat	Riyal	Oil, dates, tobacco, frankincense	1,390,000
Qatar	4,247	11,000	Doha	Riyal	Oil	340,000
Saudi Arabia	830,060	2,149,690	Riyadh	Riyal	Oil	12,680,000
United Arab Emirates	32,280	83,600	Abu Dhabi	Dirhan	Oil, gas	1,450,000
Yemen, North	75,295	195,000	San'a	Riyal	Cotton, coffee, hides	6,900,000
Yemen, South	128,569	332,968	Aden	Dinar	Cotton, fish, refined oil	2,490,000

▲ *High, dry mountains surround the fertile tableland of the Yemen.*

The world's most powerful cartel is the Organization of Petroleum Exporting Countries (OPEC), made up of Arab nations and others. Since 1973, when OPEC quadrupled the price of oil, it has had a near monopoly in the export of oil.

teachings to the rest of the world. The religious journey soon turned into a quest for territory. The Muslims (followers of Islam) defeated Iraq and Persia; spread into India, Africa, Spain, and France; and even took some Byzantine territory. This huge Arab Empire stood until 1258, when Mongols (tribes from eastern Asia) swept through, killing whole populations and leveling whole cities.

Muslim scholars were not interested in the time before Muhammad, and they wrote little or nothing about those thousands of years of Arab history. In fact, some Muslims destroyed early records.

After the year 1258, Arabians lived mostly in poverty and isolated from the West. Their glorious past was little known to Western historians. In the 1800's, archeologists began to find ruins. The ruins of huge cities, long and broad avenues, canals, and dams that have been uncovered tell of an ancient, complex Arabian civilization. And today, even the poorest Arabians

have a complicated system of hospitality and social relations that comes from a deep-felt responsibility for every action. This system comes not from the harsh life of the desert, but from an earlier, more prosperous time.

Countries of Arabia Arabia has been thought of as a distinct geographical area since ancient times. The Romans thought of Arabia as a three-part region: *Arabia Felix* (an independently ruled territory); *Arabia Petrae* (which was ruled by Rome); and *Arabia Deserta* (which was ruled by Persia). Until the coming of Muhammad and the founding of the Islamic religion, the history of Arabia was the history of many peoples and many rulers.

From the 1500's much of Arabia was under Turkish rule. But by World War I Turkish control had become weak, and by 1927 the kingdom of Saudi Arabia had come into being. Its founder was King Ibn

Saud. In 1938 oil was discovered near Dhahran, on the east coast, and this marked the beginning of a new era for Saudi Arabia. The country changed from being a little-known desert kingdom of wandering tribes into one of the world's richest nations, as a result of pumping oil from beneath the sands.

The other countries of Arabia are much smaller than Saudi Arabia. In the southwest are the two Yemens: North Yemen (the Yemen Arab Republic or Yemen San'a), and South Yemen (the Yemen People's Democratic Republic). The port of Aden in South Yemen is located on a key strategic position, at the mouth of the Red Sea.

To the east is the independent *sultanate* (a state ruled by a sultan, who is a ruler of a Muslim country) of Oman, which has a fertile coastal strip but a dry and desolate interior. Beyond the Strait of Hormuz lies the Persian (or Arabian) Gulf. Along its shores are the countries of the United Arab Emirates (a federation of seven states ruled by a prince, or *emir*). The seven are Abu Dhabi, Dubai, Ajman, Sharjah, Umm al Qawain, Fujairah, and Ras al Khaimah. They were for-

merly known as the Trucial States and, like other states in the Gulf, were protected by Britain until Britain withdrew from the Gulf in the 1970's.

The remaining two independent nations of Arabia are Qatar, an *emirate* (a nation ruled by an emir) on the Gulf next to the United Arab Emirates, and Kuwait, which is an island sheikdom at the northern tip of the Gulf. (*Sheik* is an Arabic word meaning "ruler.")

Oil revenues have helped finance extensive modernization and development of agriculture and industry in all these countries. Only the two Yemens are not rich in oil.

Arabian Life   Arabs are bound together by a common language, common customs and traditions, and a common faith—Islam. Religion is especially important in the lives of most Arabs. Each Muslim tries once in his lifetime to travel to the holy city of Mecca in western Saudi Arabia.

While some Arabs now prefer to wear Western clothes, many Arabs still wear traditional clothing, designed to protect them from the heat and cold of the desert, even when living in modern cities. Arab women

▲ *Arabia is a region of desert. But the oil hidden beneath the desert sand has made Arabia wealthy.*

◀ *The oil industry has changed the Arabs' way of life. It has made Arabia a center of modern trade and a political region of great significance.*

▶ *A Bedouin Arab outside his tent home. Despite the changes in Arabia, many Arabs still lead a nomadic life, herding sheep and goats.*

commonly wear long robes and veil their faces in most Arabian countries. Muslim law allows a man to have up to four wives. But nowadays few Arabs take more than one wife. Women are gaining greater freedom in Arab life, largely because of growing prosperity and better education. In their homes, many rich women wear gorgeous silks and jewelry. A sheik wears an *abba*, a woolen cloak. A long, white cotton shirt is worn under an abba. The head covering, a *ghoutra*, is a square, cotton cloth folded in a triangle and held in place by woolen cords.

ALSO READ: ARABIC, DESERT, ISLAM, MIDDLE EAST, MUHAMMAD, SAUDI ARABIA.

ARABIAN NIGHTS The stories of Ali Baba and the Forty Thieves, Aladdin's Lamp, Sindbad the Sailor, and the Magic Carpet are world-famous. Each is from an exciting story in the *Arabian Nights*. This collection of ancient folk tales is often called *A Thousand and One Nights*. The stories were first written in Arabic, but the earliest ones came from Persia, India, and Turkey. The author is unknown.

The legend of how the stories were first told is a story in itself. Once upon a time, there was a Persian king,

Shariar, who hated women. He would marry a different woman each night. The next morning he would have his new queen killed. He finally chose as his queen Scheherazade, who was as wise as she was lovely.

Every night she told the king an exciting story. But she never finished a tale the same night as she started it. The king was so interested in the stories he let Scheherazade live to tell the endings. By the time 1,001 nights had passed and 1,001 stories had been told, the king liked Scheherazade as much as her stories. She remained his wife and his queen forever.

ALSO READ: ARABIA, FOLKLORE, GENIE, LEGEND, MAGIC MYTHOLOGY.

ARABIC Over 130 million people in northern Africa and the Middle East speak Arabic. The Arabic alphabet has 28 characters formed by dots and curlicues. All the letters stand for

▼ *According to the legend, Scheherazade delighted the king so much with her 1,001 stories of the Arabian Nights that he spared her life and made her his queen forever.*

بِسْمِ اللّٰهِ الرّحْمٰنِ الرّحِيْمِ ①

اللّٰهُ لَا إِلٰهَ إِلَّا هُوَ الْحَيُّ الْقَيُّوْمُ ③

An example of Arabic writing. In English it means "In the name of Allah, the gracious, the merciful Allah, there is no other God but him, the Immortal. . ."

consonants, and the shape of each letter depends on its position in a word. Arabic is written from right to left. The oldest known Arabic writing dates from A.D. 512, but the exact origin of Arabic is not clear.

The Koran, the ancient holy book of the Islamic religion, was written in Arabic. Through the years people studied the Koran and closely copied its style of writing. Written Arabic changed very little. But, as people spoke to each other, spoken Arabic gradually changed until it is now very different from written Arabic. Another form of Arabic has developed in recent years. Modern Arabic is used in newspapers, books, radio, and television, to discuss new things and ideas that did not exist during the time when the Koran was written.

Arabic belongs to a group of languages called *Semitic* languages. Other major Semitic languages spoken today are Hebrew and Amharic (the Ethiopian language). Ancient Semitic languages that are no longer spoken include Phoenician and Aramaic, the language of Jesus.

For an idea of how Arabic sounds, imagine a new boy coming to school in Syria. He may say to his classmates, *"Sabah il-khayr"* (pronounced: sah-BAH il KEER), meaning "Good morning." Then he may say: *"Ismi Ahmad"* (is-MEE ah-MAHD), "My name is Ahmad."

ALSO READ: ALPHABET, HEBREW, KORAN, LANGUAGES, NUMBER, WRITTEN LANGUAGE.

ARAL SEA The Aral Sea lies in the southern part of the Soviet Union. This sea is really a giant lake, about the size of West Virginia. It is the fourth largest lake in the world, and the second largest in Asia (after the Caspian Sea). It has an area of 24,750 square miles (64,100 sq. km) and contains more than 300 small islands. (See the map with the article on SOVIET UNION.)

Because the Aral Sea contains many islands, the Russians named it *Aralskoye more* ("sea of islands").

The Aral Sea is fed by two rivers, the Syr Darya and Amu Darya. Water that flows into the rivers comes from snow and rain running off mountains far to the south. These rivers flow across miles of desert and finally collect in the Aral Sea. Farmers use water from the rivers to irrigate their crops. The water in the Aral Sea is slightly salty because it was once connected with the Caspian Sea, the largest lake in the world, which lies to the west.

Farmers who live near the Aral Sea raise cotton. Fishing, once important, has suffered from the effects of water pollution. The area is developing as an industrial zone. Sodium and magnesium deposits are mined on the Aral's shores.

ALSO READ: CASPIAN SEA, IRRIGATION, LAKE, SOVIET UNION.

ARBORETUM see BOTANICAL GARDEN.

The Arabs of long ago made important discoveries in mathematics. Our words "zero" and "algebra" are from Arabic, as are our number symbols such as 1, 2, and 3.

In many places, as buildings fall down over the centuries, other buildings are put up in the same place. This raises the ground level. People excavating all over modern London have found that today's city is 20 feet (6 m) higher in places than the old Roman town.

▼ *Archeologists learn much from aerial photography. Seen from above, the outlines of long-hidden ruins, tracks, or farms are revealed by the camera.*

ARCHEOLOGY Thousands of years from now, something you own may be found by a person called an *archeologist*. It might be a toy, a belt buckle, a dish, or part of your house. By studying the find and testing it, that archeologist may learn a lot about you and how you have lived. Archeology is the scientific study of the remains of past civilizations, or ways of life.

The bits and pieces left by ancient peoples can tell archeologists many things. Foundations of buildings and ruins of temples help them know what ancient cities looked like. Objects they find are called *artifacts*. These may be coins, tools, jewelry, or potsherds (bits of pottery). Tools, baskets, and pottery all tell something about everyday life. Human bones can tell what ancient people looked like. Animal bones tell what kinds of animals ancient peoples kept, killed, or ate. Archeologists are much like modern-day detectives, eagerly collecting clues and using all their skills to solve a mystery.

Many of the objects discovered will have been cast aside as rubbish by

▲ *Archeology is a slow, patient science. Workers on a site remove soil very carefully. They set out a numbered grid, marked by strings. Each find is marked to record exactly where it was found. Photographs and drawings are made at intervals as the work goes on.*

their owners and so are often broken. Complete objects, and sometimes rare and valuable ones, are more often found in graves, where they have been placed for use by their owners after death. Archeologists must always remember that what is left for them to discover may not tell the whole story of earlier ages. Much will have been lost, including objects made of cloth, leather, basketwork, or wood. These are preserved only in very dry or very wet conditions. Unless durable remains have also been left behind, the picture put together by an archeologist will always be incomplete.

Choosing a "Dig"　How do archeologists know where to look for buried cities? In the past, they could only guess, by using old maps, legends, the Bible, and ancient historical writings. These gave them hints and some facts as to where to look for remains of ancient civilizations. They might even begin to dig where a farmer had found an old clay pot while plowing a field.

Archeologists today use new methods, such as *aerial photography*. They take pictures from a plane flying over an area thought to have been a lost city. These pictures show shapes that cannot be seen from the ground. Old trenches and walls show up in photographs, hinting where an old city might be buried. When a trench or wall is spotted, the archeologist and a crew go to the place to excavate, or dig. *Underwater exploration* is another way to find things from the past. An archeologist wearing an aqualung can search for sunken treasure in deep waters.

Ancient peoples often built cities on top of older, decayed ones. Many layers, called *strata*, made at different times may be in one site, underneath each other. Archeologists very carefully and slowly dig down through the

▲ *The remains of the ancient city of Troy in Asia Minor. The city was discovered by the German archeologist, Heinrich Schliemann.*

◄ *Divers wearing aqualungs can explore ancient wrecks. Sometimes they find long-lost cargoes of wine and oil jars. Occasionally divers find a treasure ship.*

◄ *Burial sites are of interest to archeologists because ancient peoples often buried objects with the dead. These objects were for the dead person's use in the next world. Such remains, and the bones themselves, tell us much about life long ago.*

▶ *The tomb of the Chinese emperor Ch'in-shih-Huang (died 210 B.C.) contained around 6,000 life-size pottery figures of warriors and horses. More than 700,000 convicts took 38 years to build the tomb!*

When Mount Vesuvius erupted in A.D. 79 the cities of Pompeii and Herculaneum were completely covered by ash, stones, and mud to a depth of about 12 feet (4 m). Excavations to uncover the cities began in the 18th century and are still going on. Unlike the objects found in most excavations, those at Pompeii and Herculaneum are usually in good condition. Even the *graffiti*, or scribblings on the walls, can still be read. "Successus the cloth-weaver loves Iris, the innkeeper's slave," or "I am surprised, O wall, that you have not fallen down with the weight of all this scribbled rubbish."

layers, keeping accurate records all the while. It is most important that archeologists record exactly where an object was found, and what other objects were found near it, in order to know the *context* of a find. Then they can build up a sequence of events in the correct order. If a single object is removed, or a site disturbed, this valuable evidence of the order in which objects were buried will be destroyed. Archeologists seek the help of other experts to discover all they can about an object. Botanists identify plants from which preserved pollen grains, seeds, or even charred wood originally came. This can give a picture of what earlier landscapes looked like, what plants grew, what people ate, and what crops they grew. Zoologists can give similar evidence from animal remains. Geologists can find out where building stone came from, for example. Physicists can give a date for objects by using various radioactive dating methods. Many archeologists work for museums which display the things they find.

Careful records were not always kept when people first became interested in learning about the past. Bits of pots and bones and other ancient

objects were often destroyed. Some diggers kept only treasures and pretty things, not knowing how important every artifact might be. Today, however, archeologists preserve every single clue they can find in their study of ancient times.

Relics of life in ancient times have been found all over the world—in the ruins of Pompeii and Troy, in old sailing ships sunk in the Aegean and Mediterranean seas, in the tomb of Egyptian King Tutankhamun, in caves near the Dead Sea, in underground rooms built by Indians. Lost cities and civilizations may still be buried beneath oceans, covered by centuries of rebuilding, or hidden beneath the earth.

ALSO READ: ANCIENT CIVILIZATIONS, ANTHROPOLOGY.

ARCHERY Shooting arrows from a bow is called archery. It was invented thousands of years ago for hunting and warfare. Today it is a popular sport.

Bows and arrows can be dangerous. So a beginner must be taught to handle them correctly and safely by

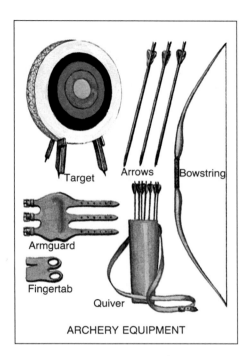

Target · Arrows · Bowstring

Armguard

Fingertab

Quiver

ARCHERY EQUIPMENT

an experienced archer.

Before buying a bow, an archer should know the bow's *draw weight*, or how hard the string must be drawn, or pulled, to shoot the arrow. Draw weights range from 15 to 75 pounds (7 to 34 kg). Bows with low draw weights are for young or beginning archers. Bows from 25 to 45 pounds (11 to 20 kg) are used in tournaments, or shooting contests. Bows today are made of either fiberglass or wood. Bowstrings are usually made of Dacron.

Arrows come in different lengths and thicknesses. An archer picks different size arrows for different purposes. The rear end of an arrow, the *nock*, has a slot that fits around the bowstring. In front of the nock are feathers, called *vanes*. Vanes make the arrow fly straight. The long body of the arrow is the *shaft*, which ends in a metal arrowpoint.

An archer wears a *tab*, or shooting glove, on the hand that grips the bow. An *armguard* protects his fingers and wrist when the bowstring snaps back as an arrow is shot. A *quiver*, or case, holds the arrows.

A right-handed archer holds the middle of the bow with the left hand.

He or she uses three fingers of the right hand to hold the bowstring and arrow. The arrow nock fits between the index and middle fingers. The arrowshaft goes against the left side of the bow. The archer draws the bow, pulling the hand back until the index finger touches the jaw, directly below the eye. This spot on the face is the *anchor point*. The archer aims at the target, and then releases the arrow by relaxing the fingers. Never snap the fingers to release the arrow.

Many nations send archers to world championship competitions and the Olympics. *Target archers* shoot at 48-inch (1.2-m) circle targets, called *butts*. *Field archers* shoot at much smaller butts. Both shoot from various distances.

ALSO READ: BOW AND ARROW, OLYMPIC GAMES, SPORTS.

There is a form of archery in which the archer tries to shoot his or her arrow as far as possible. It is called *flight shooting*. In free-style flight shooting the archer lies on his back with the bow strapped to his feet. Both hands are thus free to draw the very heavy bow. In this class of shooting, distances of well over a mile (1.6 km) are achieved.

▼ *Archery is a sport requiring skill and practice. The archer must learn how to stand and how to hold the bow and arrow correctly for accurate aiming, drawing, and release.*

▲ *Archimedes, scientist and inventor of ancient Greece.*

ARCHIMEDES (about 287–212 B.C.) Archimedes is called the "father of experimental science." He was perhaps the first of thousands of patient inventors who have spent years proving their ideas by experiment. Among other things, this Greek mathematician and inventor discovered how to use levers and pulleys to lift heavy objects, and how to pump water uphill.

Archimedes spent most of his life in the Greek colony of Syracuse, in Sicily. He designed war machines for his king. The machines helped the king hold off an enemy invasion for three years, but Archimedes is said to have been killed during the final battle for the city.

The king of Syracuse once asked Archimedes to tell him if his new crown was pure gold. Archimedes thought of how to test the crown when he stepped into a full bathtub and watched it overflow. His body displaced (moved) a certain amount of water. So a crown of pure gold should displace the same amount of water as a chunk of pure gold weighing the same as the crown. Archimedes was so excited by his discovery that he rushed naked from his bath, shouting "Eureka!" (I have found it!) When he performed the test, Archimedes found that the crown was not pure gold. The goldsmith had cheated the king.

ALSO READ: BUOYANCY; GREECE, ANCIENT; MACHINE; PHYSICS; SCIENCE.

ARCHITECTURE Architecture is the art of designing and constructing buildings. The person who does this work is an *architect*. A painter tries to arrange materials in a beautiful way, and so does an architect. But architects must do more than design beautiful buildings. They must be able to plan useful buildings, and they must know practical ways to build them. In school, architects learn artistic design, drawing, and the history of art. They also study mathematics and construction methods. After graduating, students enter an architect's office and help in the many jobs necessary to produce complete building plans. At first they are given very simple jobs to do, but as they learn further they are given more responsibility. Finally, the state may license architects, allowing them to start their own offices.

▶ *Archimedes is said to have invented this screw machine for raising water for irrigation. By turning the handle at the top, the screw rotates inside a cylinder. Water trapped in the screw is lifted from the lower level to the higher.*

Architectural Styles

Egyptian	4000 B.C.	Pyramids, tombs, temples.
Chinese	1000 B.C.	Palaces, pagodas, the Great Wall.
Greek	300 B.C.	Graceful pillars and columns, temples, theaters.
Roman	200 B.C. to A.D. 400	Arches, aqueducts, amphitheaters, roads, villas with central heating.
Byzantine	A.D. 300's to 1400's	Ornate churches with dome rising from square base. Brickwork, pillars and mosaics.
Roman-esque	A.D. 1100	Norman cathedrals, castles. Stone arches.
Gothic	1200	Vaulted roofs, high spires, buttressed walls. Includes English Decorated and Perpendicular styles.
Renaissance	1400	Modeled on Greek and Roman.
Baroque	1600	Ornate, decorated, three dimensional.
Georgian and Neo-Classical	1700's and 1800's	Terraces of town houses, country mansions, elegant plaster ceilings. Imitated Greek and Roman. Examples are Jefferson's house at Monticello and Supreme Court building in Washington, D.C.
Modern	1900's	Steel-frame, glass-walled, skyscrapers. Examples are the Empire State Building and the World Trade Center in New York, Sears Tower in Chicago and John Hancock Building in Boston.

ARCHITECTURE THROUGH THE AGES

Greek Doric: Temple of Neptune, Greece

Roman: Arch of Constantine, Rome, Italy

Byzantine: Santa Sophia, Istanbul, Turkey

Gothic: Bourges Cathedral, France

Renaissance: Florence Cathedral, Italy

Modern: Empire State Building, New York, USA

Modern: Sydney Opera House, Sydney, Australia

ARCHITECTURE

▶ *The citadel of Aleppo in Syria was built to be the strongest fortress in the Arab world. Its architects designed it for both strength and beauty.*

Doric

Ionic

Corinthian

▲ *Three types of columns with their carved capitals. These styles were used by the early Greeks.*

One of America's greatest contributions to architecture is the skyscraper. The tallest of these steel, concrete, and glass giants is the Sears Tower in Chicago, Illinois. It is 1,454 feet (443 m) high and has 110 stories. More than 16,000 people work in the building. There are 103 elevators and 16,000 windows.

Buildings today are sometimes so large and complicated that one architect cannot do all the work. These buildings—skyscrapers, for example—are usually planned by a team of architects and others in a large office. In addition to the architect for the building and the drafters who help draw the plans, there may be a structural engineer to help design the frame, a mechanical engineer to design the heating and air conditioning, a representative on the building site, and so on.

Materials, Moods, and Styles
When an architect first starts to plan a building, he or she must be very sure of what its purpose and size will be. Does a school need a big auditorium? Will families with several children live in an apartment house? Does an airplane factory need extra-large rooms and doors? Will an office building serve the needs of different kinds of workers? The architect must also consider the building materials and construction methods available. What materials and workmanship can the client afford? How will steelwork last in a humid climate? Do local fire laws allow wood shingles? What kind of foundation is needed to support a building on swampy ground? All these important questions must be answered.

Good architecture is not only practical. It creates certain moods. A high ceiling makes a room look spacious. A tall house roof suggests shelter. Heavy, rugged masonry suggests durability and toughness. To give a building the right character or mood, an architect must plan the effect that a building will have from the outside as well as from the inside. Some architects design furniture so that it will match the design of the rooms. Many architects design a setting of parks or streets for buildings. These *landscape architects* are usually gardeners, too. The way a building looks is called its *style*. A building's style can tell us about the architect's personality, because architects use shapes and colors they like.

Good architecture reflects the needs and way of life of its times. In times when life was easy, architects often used large windows to flood rooms with sparkling light. During hard times, people wanted thick walls and blocky shapes that made them feel safe. Architecture has changing fashions. Throughout history, there have been numerous fashions, or styles—such as Romanesque, Gothic, Baroque, Contemporary, and so on.

Look at the buildings pictured with this article. How different they all are. Yet they were all designed by architects. They wanted their buildings to be beautiful as well as useful. The spire of the Gothic cathedral soared high above the rest of the town, just as today the tall skyscrapers downtown dwarf other smaller buildings in the city. Did you know that some of the great European cathedrals took hundreds of years to build?

The Cutlers' Guildhall in England (see next page) was built during the Middle Ages. It has a wooden framework with plastered walls. Notice the small windows. And can you see how the second floor is wider than the first floor? Underneath the building is an open space, which was probably used as a meeting place.

Filippo Brunelleschi began the Church of San Lorenzo in Florence, Italy, in 1421: This was during the period called the *Renaissance* (the rebirth of knowledge). Brunelleschi was the first Renaissance architect. His style shows the interest Renaissance people had in science. The walls and ceiling of the church are flat. Straight lines and perfect circles make up the floor tiles, ceiling beams, and windows. The gray marble columns and windows stand out clearly from the white walls. All of these parts of Brunelleschi's design show that he did not want his building to be surprising. Instead, he made his design very regular, so that people could quickly see each part and be impressed by the clear, sharp shapes.

Architects sometimes must finish or remodel old buildings. The Church of St. Peter in Rome was

▶ *Medieval builders at work high on the spire of a Gothic cathedral. These tall towers depended on firm foundations. They were built as a sign that people on earth were reaching upward to heaven.*

▲ *The Church of San Lorenzo, in Florence, Italy.*

▲ *The Eiffel Tower, in Paris, France.*

but still be safe. Gustave Eiffel, an engineer, proved that very tall buildings can be made of strong metal. The Eiffel Tower, built for the Paris World's Fair of 1889, and 984 feet (300 m) high, was made of iron.

Modern Architecture Louis Sullivan, an American architect, felt that tall buildings ought to rise as simple rectangles rather than be complicated in form, as most buildings were in 1890 or even later. He loved ornament, but used it more carefully than previous architects did, to keep the basic design simple. He designed the Schlesinger and Meyer Department Store in Chicago, between 1899 and 1904. This early department store's straight lines and plain walls clearly show it is built of steel and glass. However, thick walls of brick and stone supports hold up the floors and roof. Another construction method is used for modern steel buildings. All the beams and columns are fastened together into a single framework.

begun in 1506, and several great architects worked on it for over a century. In 1623, Giovanni Bernini, the greatest architect of the 1600's, was asked to complete the church. He worked for more than 50 years. No other architect has ever worked on one project for so long a time. Bernini fitted the work of the earlier architects into his own complicated design, and he made St. Peter's the beautiful and inspiring church we see today.

By the middle 1800's, new materials and inventions were used in designing buildings. As cities became more crowded, architects had to get more people onto less ground space. After the first safety elevator was invented in 1853, architects could save ground space by designing *skyscrapers*—buildings much taller than any built before. Modern steel and concrete are stronger than wood, brick, or stone. So modern buildings can be much higher than earlier buildings

▼ *The medieval Cutlers' Guildhall at Thaxted, in England.*

Then the walls and floors are hung on this framework, just like paper on a kite frame. Walter Gropius, a German architect, made dramatic use of this construction method. He did not hide the steel skeleton behind solid walls. Instead, in one of his buildings he hung thin glass walls from the roof like a curtain. This building was the Bauhaus, an art school that Gropius built in Germany in 1925 and 1926. The glass walls allow daylight to enter every part of the art studio. The steel framework and conrete floors can be seen inside this glass shell. Many offices and factories also have glass walls to let light inside and to let the workers have an outside view.

Le Corbusier, a Swiss architect, helped design the United Nations building in New York. He also built a mountaintop church in France in the 1950's. This concrete church, with its curved roof and walls, and tiny windows and hidden doors, seems to grow out of the ground. Le Corbusier used concrete shapes to express the moods of his buildings—using them to create a mood of safety and trust in a church, for instance.

Ludwig Mies van der Rohe, a Ger-

man-American, planned even the smallest details of his buildings. His Seagram Building in New York City was built in 1957. Every beam and window is exactly related in size and color to every other part of the build-

▲ *The Schlesinger and Meyer Department Store (now Carson Pirie Scott & Company) in Chicago, Illinois, designed by Louis Sullivan.*

▼ *The Bauhaus Workshop in Dessau, Germany.*

The world's tallest *tower* is the CN Tower in Metro Center, Toronto, Canada. It is 1,822 feet (555 m) high and lightning strikes it almost 200 times every year without doing any damage.

ing. The Seagram Building is lively and interesting all the time. During the day, its glass walls reflect the movements of the clouds and city around it. At night, lights and people inside make this office building seem to come alive. Mies van der Rohe influenced many later architects because his designs are so interesting.

Today, as well as experimenting with new styles and construction materials, architects are very concerned about making the right kinds of buildings for people to live, work, and play in.

■ LEARN BY DOING

An architect has to answer many questions in designing a building. Suppose you try designing a new house for your family. Answer these questions. How can your house be friendly? Quiet? How many rooms does your family need? What rooms? How many bedrooms? Where will the trash be collected? What will the kitchen be like? Will there be a driveway? If you want your house to feel friendly, will you use little windows and heavy, rough stone blocks? If you want it to feel quiet and safe, will you use soft colors and shapes that are not surprising? What materials will you use? Wood? Glass? Plastic? Think about the space around the house. Will you have a garden?

Try making two models of your house, one of clay and one of cardboard. Do the two models feel different to you? What difference does coloring make? All these are questions an architect must answer every time he or she designs a building. ■

For further information on:
Ancient Architecture, *see* ABU SIMBEL, ACROPOLIS, PYRAMID, SPHINX.

◀ *The Sears Tower in Chicago is the world's tallest building. It was completed in 1974.*

Architects, *see* MICHELANGELO; WRIGHT, FRANK LLOYD.

Design and Construction, *see* BRIDGE, BUILDING MATERIAL, CAISSON, CASTLE, CATHEDRAL, CONCRETE, CONSTRUCTION, EMPIRE STATE BUILDING, GOTHIC ARCHITECTURE, HOUSE, LEANING TOWER OF PISA, PAGODA, STAINED GLASS, TEMPLE.

History, *see* BAROQUE PERIOD, RENAISSANCE, ROCOCO ART, ROMANESQUE ART.

ARCTIC Around the North Pole lies an imaginary line known as the Arctic Circle. Can you find it on a globe? (On globes and maps it is drawn at 66½ degrees north lati-tude—almost exactly three-fourths of the distance from the equator to the North Pole.) North of this line, tem-peratures are very low for much of the year. In winter it can be as cold as minus 90°F (−68°C), though even this is not so cold as at the South Pole. Even in summer the average temper-ature is no more than 50°F (10°C). Always-frozen soil, called *permafrost*, lies below the surface of the land. The region is so cold that trees are dwarfed and in places grow only inches high. Few things can live in this bitterly cold, barren region.

In the Arctic are the northernmost parts of Alaska, Canada, the U.S.S.R., Norway, Sweden, and Finland; most of Greenland, the larg-

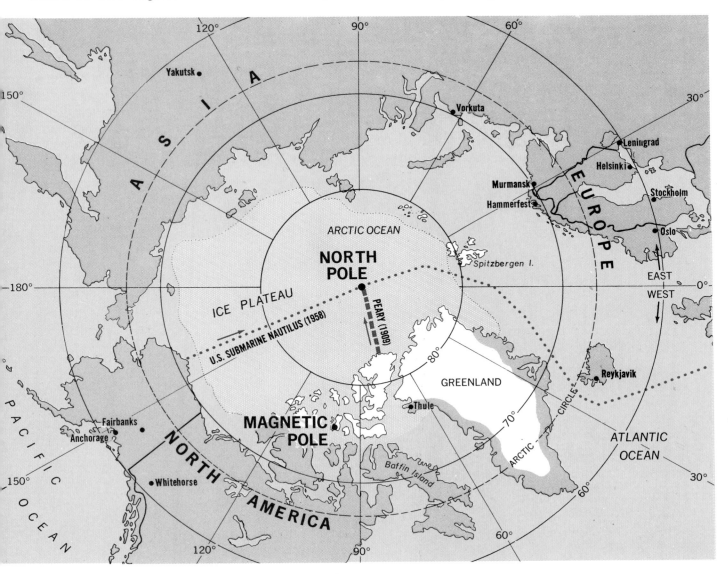

The Arctic town of Verkhoyansk in Siberia holds the record for the greatest range of temperature between winter and summer. It has had a winter temperature of −90°F (−68°C) and a hottest summer temperature of 98°F (36.7°C). Can you figure out this frightening difference in temperature in degrees Fahrenheit?

est island in the world; many smaller islands; and the Arctic Ocean. About two million people live within the Arctic Circle. Of these people, some 450,000 are native peoples such as Eskimos (Inuit), Indians, and Lapps. The largest Arctic city is Murmansk in the U.S.S.R.

Filling a Hole The Arctic regions of North America do not touch those of Europe and Asia. The almost circular space around the North Pole holds the Arctic Ocean. Nearly all year a layer of ice, which is thicker than a man is tall, floats on most of the ocean. This "ice hat" is made up of huge chunks of ice called the *polar ice pack*. The ice is slowly pushed in a circle by ocean currents and winds. The Earth's spin on its axis mainly causes the circular movement of the ocean.

The Arctic Ocean is the smallest of the Earth's oceans. The mean depth of the ocean is about 4,000 feet (1,220 m). The ocean covers 5,440,000 square miles (14,090,000 sq. km), including its many seas and bays.

This is about the same size as the continent of Antarctica. The Lomonosov Ridge, an undersea mountain range, has peaks that rise as high as 9,000 feet (2,740 m) from the ocean floor. But the ocean is deep in this region—more than 2,500 feet (762 m) of water cover even the highest peak. Deep basins separate many peaks.

■ **LEARN BY DOING**

Fill a shallow saucer almost full of water on a freezing cold winter day. Set it outside on a flat surface. Come back in an hour and take a look. Has ice formed on the water's surface? When ice chunks and chips form, blow them about. See how the ice bunches, piles up, crowds under, and rumples. You are holding a miniature model of the Arctic Ocean and its shifting, drifting ice. ■

The Arctic Ocean's "hat" of ice is worn a little to one side. In summer it reaches about 1,200 miles (1,930 km) from the North Pole down the Pacific Ocean side of the Earth. But the ice extends only half that distance down

▶ *A massive castlelike iceberg in the Arctic. Such icebergs form when chunks of ice fall into the sea from the tip of a valley glacier.*

MAJOR EVENTS IN THE ARCTIC

330 B.C.	Pytheas, probably the first Arctic explorer, discovered Iceland.
A.D. 982	Eric the Red discovered Greenland.
1610	Henry Hudson discovered the strait and bay later named after him.
1728	Vitus Bering discovered the strait later named after him.
1878–79	Nils A. E. Nordenskjöld was the first to sail through the Northeast Passage.
1903–06	Roald Amundsen was the first to sail through the Northwest Passage.
1909	Robert E. Peary led the first expedition to reach the North Pole.
1926	Richard E. Byrd was the first man to fly over the North Pole.
1926	Roald Amundsen and others crossed the Arctic in a dirigible (lighter-than-air-craft).
1957–58	Scientists participating in the International Geophysical Year studied many aspects of the Arctic. Over 300 scientific stations were set up in the Arctic to study, among other things, the weather, the ice cap, and the water of the Arctic Ocean.
1958	*Nautilus,* a U.S. atomic submarine, sailed under the Arctic ice cap.
1959	*Skate,* a U.S. atomic submarine, surfaced through the ice at the North Pole, the first ship ever to do this.
1969	*Manhattan,* an enormous oil tanker, was the first large commercial ship to navigate the Northwest Passage.
1977	*Arktika,* a Soviet ice-breaker, reached the North Pole.

Although the Arctic is a cold place, it is much milder than the Antarctic. The South Pole is a desolate place, covered by ice up to two-and-a-half miles (4,000 m) thick. The North Pole temperatures are higher because of the sea just under the ice. The ice at the North Pole is only 16 feet (5 m) thick.

the Atlantic side, because warm water from the current called the Gulf Stream reaches northward through the Atlantic Ocean.

Some pack ice stays in the Arctic Ocean for years, melting a bit in summer and growing bigger again the following winter. Giant sheets of pack ice buckle and break when they push together. Then one large flat piece of ice, or *floe*, slides up over another. The surface crinkles like a plowed field. Channels, called *leads*, open in the ice sheet. Leads made dog-sled travel dangerous for Robert E. Peary, who led the first trip to the North Pole, in 1909.

Sailors in the Arctic The period from 1400 to 1879 was one of exploration around the edge of the polar ice pack. Explorers searched for fur-bearing animals and for minerals. They tried to find a "Northeast Passage" that would lead a ship from Europe to Asia, and a "Northwest Passage" that would lead a ship north from the east coast to the west coast of the United States. William Baffin sailed the waters west of Greenland in 1616. The Bering Strait, a water passage that separates Alaska and Sibe-

ria, was discovered by Vitus Bering in 1728. Nils Nordenskjöld sailed first through the Northeast Passage (1878–79), and Roald Amundsen was the first to sail through the Northwest Passage (1903–06).

U.S. Navy atomic-powered submarine *Nautilus* became the first ship to reach the North Pole undersea. It traveled more than 1,800 miles (2,897 km) beneath the Arctic ice cap in four days in 1958. The submarine *Skate* became the first to surface at the pole in 1959. These journeys opened the possibility of future undersea commercial travel beneath the Arctic ice cap.

Planes of many countries fly over

▼ *The Arctic is "the land of the midnight sun." At midsummer the sun never sets. Even at midnight it is still just above the horizon.*

▲ *Most of Greenland lies within the Arctic Circle. The short Arctic summer brings out many tundra plants, which bloom quickly in the long, sunny days.*

the North Pole on international flights. The shortest way between some parts of North America and Asia is over the Arctic Ocean. There are weather stations and defense installations in the Arctic. Cargo ships plow through the Northeast Passage each summer. They sail along the coast of Siberia from Norway. Icebreakers clear channels in the ice. The ships load lumber, graphite, and reindeer skins at Arctic ports. Finally, the ships reach the Bering Sea. Few ships break their way through the Northwest Passage in northern Canada, although a huge oil tanker, *Manhattan*, navigated this route in 1969. Vast oil deposits have been discovered in the Alaskan Arctic and a pipeline across Alaska was completed in 1977.

ALSO READ: AMUNDSEN, ROALD; BERING, VITUS; BYRD, RICHARD E.; HUDSON, HENRY; LAPLAND; NORTH POLE; NORTHWEST PASSAGE; PEARY, ROBERT; POLAR LIFE; TUNDRA.

ARGENTINA Argentina is the second largest country of South America. With its grassy *pampas* (prairie), its snow-capped Andes Mountains, and its wild, windy southern plateau, it is a large, beauti-

ful country of contrasts. (See the map with the article on SOUTH AMERICA.)

About one-third of the Argentine people live in and around Buenos Aires. It is the largest city and most important port in South America. From there, the pampas—the vast, treeless, grassy plain—spreads out fanlike for 300 to 400 miles (480 to 640 km). Argentina's economy depends almost entirely on the rich, fertile soil of the pampas. Raising beef

▼ *Argentina's pampas, or plains, are ideal for ranching cattle, as well as growing wheat.*

ARGENTINA

Capital City: Buenos Aires (3,000,000 people).
Area: 1,068,379 square miles (2,766,889 sq. km).
Population: 32,600,000.
Government: Republic.
Main Products: Meat and meat products, wheat, textiles, leather, machinery.
Unit of Money: Peso.
Official Language: Spanish.

cattle is its main industry. Argentina is one of the world leaders in production of beef and hides. Wheat, corn, and flax are also grown in the pampas. Argentina is now one of the greatest wheat-producing areas of the world. In the 1800's, nomadic cowboys, the *gauchos*, herded cattle over the unfenced pampas. But in the late 1800's, a few rich men bought up the grazing lands and fenced in the pampas to raise cattle on huge ranches called *estancias*. The old way of life of the gauchos is gradually disappearing.

Northern Argentina is mostly the *Gran Chaco*, a partly swampy and forested lowland that borders on Paraguay and Bolivia. Southern Argentina is known as *Patagonia*, a dry, windswept plateau region with some forests and grasslands. The climate in the south is harsh, with heavy rainfall and violent winds.

Most of Argentina's Indians live in Patagonia, where sheep raising is the main occupation. Cattle cannot feed on the coarse grasses here. Some of the world's largest sheep ranches are on the island of Tierra del Fuego at Argentina's southern tip. Sheep wool is a major export.

Argentina has an oil industry, and its factories produce textiles, chemicals, and machinery. About three-fourths of the country's people live in the towns.

The highest mountain in the Western Hemisphere, Mount Aconcagua

(22,834 feet: 6,960 m), is in the Argentine Andes Mountains, which separate Argentina from Chile. People in the mountains grow fruit and work in mines or in the wine industry.

Juan Diaz de Solis, a Spanish navigator, claimed Argentina for Spain in 1516. The Spanish soon conquered the Indians, hoping to find their gold and silver. Spain ruled Argentina for nearly 300 years. General José de San Martin, the Argentine national hero, helped Argentina win independence in 1816. Argentina is now an independent republic. From 1946 to 1955, the president was Juan Domingo Perón, whose wife Eva was a prominent figure in the government. Perón and his third wife, Isabel, ruled again briefly in the 1970's. The military has taken control of the government at various times. In 1982 Argentina went briefly to war with Great Britain over the disputed Falkland Islands.

ALSO READ: ANDES MOUNTAINS; BUENOS AIRES; PERON, JUAN AND EVA; SOUTH AMERICA; SPANISH HISTORY; WHEAT.

ARGONAUT see JASON.

ARISTOTLE (384–322 B.C.) One of the greatest philosophers of all time was Aristotle of ancient Greece. He was the student of another great phi-

▲ *Aristotle, ancient Greek philosopher and teacher.*

Aristotle was one of the first persons to state that the world was round. But he wasn't correct in everything he said. He declared, for instance, that a heavy stone would fall to the ground more quickly than a light one. Everyone accepted this without question until Galileo proved it wrong two thousand years later.

▼ *John Napier, the Scottish mathematician, invented logarithms. In 1617 he explained how small rods or "bones" could be used to multiply or divide.*

losopher, Plato. Aristotle joined Plato's school in Athens when he was 18. He stayed there until Plato died, 20 years later.

Aristotle became well known as a philosopher during those years. In 342 B.C., King Philip of Macedonia called Aristotle to teach his son, Alexander, who would later be called Alexander the Great. Aristotle returned to Athens after seven years in Macedonia. Alexander, who had since become king, gave Aristotle money to set up his own school, the *Lyceum*. Aristotle studied, taught, and wrote for 12 years. Then Alexander died. The people of Athens did not like Alexander, and—because Aristotle was his friend—they did not like Aristotle. Aristotle had to leave Athens. He died the following year.

Aristotle studied and wrote about every subject known to the Greeks. Much of his writing was for his students, but only a few of his works survived. He developed the sciences of logic and physics. His ideas about zoology, politics, ethics, and literature are very important. People all over the world still read his writings.

Aristotle taught that people should act on what their study of life convinced them was right. He said the good of all was served when each person did something about what he thought and believed.

ALSO READ: ALEXANDER THE GREAT; ANCIENT CIVILIZATIONS; GREECE, ANCIENT; PHILOSOPHY; PLATO; SOCRATES.

ARITHMETIC Arithmetic is the oldest and simplest branch of mathematics. To understand what arithmetic is, we should look at how it developed. The invention of money was an important reason for the development of arithmetic. The merchants of ancient Asia, for example, bought and sold expensive goods. They had to be able to add and sub-

tract large numbers easily and accurately.

A large part of arithmetic in those times was learning how to use an *abacus*. This simple device helped a person add or subtract long lists of numbers quickly and easily.

The ancient Greeks also knew the uses of arithmetic. The word "arithmetic" comes from the Greek word *arithmos*, which means "number." For the Greeks, arithmetic had two parts. The Greeks knew all the rules for adding and subtracting, like the Asian merchants. However, they were also interested in numbers themselves. They divided numbers into many different groups. Some of these groups are easy to understand.

For example, any number that can be divided by two—such as 2, 4, 6, 8, 10, and so forth—is called an *even* number. All other numbers—1, 3, 5, 7, 9, and so forth—are called *odd* numbers. Some kinds of numbers are more difficult to understand. An interesting kind are *perfect* numbers. With every perfect number, if you add up all the numbers that divide it evenly, their sum is the number you started with. Six is a perfect number. The numbers that divide six evenly are 1, 2, and 3; and $1 + 2 + 3 = 6$. Another perfect number is 28, because $1 + 2 + 4 + 7 + 14 = 28$.

Another important advance in arithmetic came around A.D. 750, when *Arabic numerals* were first used. Arabic numerals are the numbers we use today. They are the symbols "1, 2, 3, 4, 5, 6, 7, 8, 9, 0." When we use these ten numerals, we can write even the largest numbers by combining the symbols in different ways. Many ways of writing numbers existed, but they were all complicated and hard to use. Because Arabic numerals use only ten symbols, it is fairly easy to add, subtract, multiply, and divide.

Roman numerals are another way to write numbers: 1 = I, 2 = II, 3 = III, 4 = IV, 5 = V, 6 = VI, 7 = VII, 8 = VIII, 9 = IX, 10 = X. Try adding these Roman numerals together without changing them into Arabic numerals: VI + VIII + IX = ??? See how much easier it is to use Arabic numerals.

Arithmetic still needed quick methods to solve problems. The ways to solve problems using Arabic numerals were not discovered until the 1700's. Many mathematicians helped find the rules to solve problems.

What is Arithmetic? Arithmetic is the study of how to add, subtract, multiply, and divide numbers. These are called *operations*. People who study arithmetic learn how to perform the four operations—*addition, subtraction, multiplication,* and *division.* Each of these operations has a sign—addition (+), subtraction (−), multiplication (×), and division (÷).

ADDITION. Two apples and three apples equal a total of five apples. This is a simple example of addition. Addition takes two numbers and combines them to get a third number, which is their sum. Here are more complicated examples of addition:

382	(Addend)	342
+513	(Addend)	+234
895	(Sum)	???

Each number above the line, 382 and 513, is called an *addend*. The number below the line, 895, is called the *sum*. In our example, each *digit* (numeral) in the sum can be found by adding the two numbers above it. The process is sometimes more difficult, however, when bigger numbers have to be added. Can you fill in the sum where the question marks are?

SUBTRACTION. In subtraction, you want to know the difference between two numbers. How much larger is one number than another? It is easy to see that three apples is the difference between two apples and five apples, or 5 − 2 = 3. More complicated examples are:

COMMUTATIVE LAWS: ADDITION AND MULTIPLICATION

Numbers can *commute* or change around, just as commuters go to work in the morning, then change direction and come home.

In addition: 3 sheep in a pen and 4 sheep following them gives the same result as if 4 sheep are in a pen and 3 sheep follow them.

In multiplication: 4 sets of 3 pencils is the same quantity as 3 sets of 4 pencils.

589	(Minuend)	682
− 352	(Subtrahend)	− 211
237	(Difference)	???

The large number on top, 589, is called the *minuend* in this subtraction problem. The number below it, 352, is called the *subtrahend*. The answer, 237, is called the *difference*. You can get the answer by subtracting the 3, 5, and 2, in 352, from the numbers just above them. Find the difference in the other problem. It is easy to see if your answer is correct in a subtraction problem. The subtrahend and the difference add up to the minuend number if the answer is correct. In this problem, 352 + 237 = 589, so 237 is the right answer. Was your answer to the other problem right?

MULTIPLICATION. Imagine a merchant in ancient Asia. A trader comes into the merchant's tent and offers the merchant eight chests. Four silver bowls are in each chest. How many bowls are there altogether? One

An ancient Egyptian papyrus in the British Museum is one of the most fascinating documents ever found. It is full of math problems for students, and they are exactly the sort of problems we do in school today: "A cylindrical granary is of diameter 9 and height 6. What is the amount of grain that goes into it?" or "A quantity and its ¼ added together becomes 15. What is the quantity?" This was written about 1800 B.C.

way to solve this problem would be to add 4 to itself 8 times. If you did this, you would find there are 32 silver bowls. It is easier to multiply the eight chests by four bowls in each chest:

```
      8   (Multiplicand)
     ×4   (Multiplier)
    ───
     32   (Product)
```

In this example, 8 is the *multiplicand* and 4 is the *multiplier*, which tells how many times to add 8 to itself. The answer is 32, which is the *product*. What would be the product if the merchant had 2 chests containing 6 bowls each?

DIVISION. Imagine that the trader in ancient Asia offers a merchant 32 silver bowls and 8 empty chests. The merchant wants to know how many bowls he can put in each chest after he buys all these things. One way he can find out is to put one bowl into each chest, then another and another, until he runs out of bowls. If he does this, he will have four bowls in each chest. A better way to solve the problem is to divide. The merchant would divide 8 (the number of chests) into 32 (the total number of bowls he has).

COMMON FRACTIONS
AND THEIR
DECIMAL EQUIVALENTS

$\frac{1}{8} = 0.125$
$\frac{1}{4} = 0.25$
$\frac{1}{3} = 0.333$
$\frac{1}{2} = 0.5$
$\frac{2}{3} = 0.666$
$\frac{7}{8} = 0.875$

MULTIPLICATION SQUARE

Can you see why it is easy to learn $5 \times 2, 5 \times 3, 5 \times 4 \ldots$? And still easier to learn $10 \times 2, 10 \times 3, 10 \times 4 \ldots$?

X	1	2	3	4	5	6	7	8	9	10
1										
2		4	6	8	10	12	14	16	18	20
3			9	12	15	18	21	24	27	30
4				16	20	24	28	32	36	40
5					25	30	35	40	45	50
6						36	42	48	54	60
7							49	56	63	70
8								64	72	80
9									81	90
10										100

```
        4              (Quotient)
    8 ⟌ 32   (Divisor) ⟌ (Dividend)
```

The *divisor* is 8. The *dividend* is 32, and the *quotient* is 4, the answer. It is easy to check whether you have done a division problem correctly. The divisor (8) multiplied by the quotient (4) will equal the dividend (32). The answer shown is correct in this case, because $4 \times 8 = 32$. Whenever a number divides evenly into another number, it is called a *factor*. In this example, both 4 and 8 are factors of 32, because they divide evenly into 32.

People use certain kinds of numbers to add, subtract, multiply, and divide. The numbers we used in all our examples are *whole numbers*. Whole numbers are made by adding 1 to itself any number of times. Whole numbers are called *integers*—2, 14, 137, and 1,000,000 are all integers. There are many other kinds of numbers, however.

Among the most important numbers are *fractions*. For example, a pie can be cut into four equal pieces. Each piece is a fraction, or part, of the whole pie. Each piece is one-fourth of the whole pie, or ¼. If the pie is divided into three equal parts, each piece is ⅓, or one-third, of the whole pie. The number above the line in a fraction is called the *numerator*. The one below the line is the *denominator*. Fractions can be added, subtracted, multiplied, and divided—although sometimes it is difficult to do so.

Using *decimal numbers* is a quick way to write fractions. Decimal numbers are used because they are easy to multiply and divide. The fraction ¼ is 0.25 when written as a decimal number, for example. The period in a decimal number is called a *decimal point*. The fraction ¼ is the same as 25 ÷ 100. Any fraction can be turned into a decimal fraction by dividing the numerator by the denominator.

Mathematicians took many centuries to develop the number system and arithmetic methods now used.

ALSO READ: ABACUS, DECIMAL NUMBER, EUCLID, MATHEMATICS, NUMBER.

ARIZONA Arizona (nicknamed the "Grand Canyon State," or "Apache State") is the sixth largest state in the United States. It has become one of the nation's fastest-growing areas, despite the state's deserts, mountains, and dry, empty highlands. Arizona has a rugged beauty and a healthful climate. The sun shines much of the time. The air is dry and clear. It is seldom hot in the highlands. Since the 1950's more and more people have moved to Arizona.

The Land Arizona is in the Southwest. It lies on the border of Mexico and is between California and New Mexico. The highest parts of Arizona are in the north and east, where rough highlands reach more than a mile (1.6 km) above sea level. Rivers have worn canyons out of the rock over the ages.

In central Arizona are the San Francisco Peaks, which are extinct volcanoes. They are more than 12,000 feet (3,650 m) high in places. Their tops are white with snow most of the year. Forests cover the mountainsides in central and northeastern Arizona. Pines and other trees grow there because the mountains receive enough water in the form of rain and snow. Parts of the highlands are dry most of the year. But they have rain at times. In spring and summer, grass comes up on the dry highland.

Southwestern Arizona is different from the rest of the state. It is low. There are mountains here, but most of them are not so high as those farther north. The yearly rainfall here is very light. Most of southwestern Arizona is desert or almost desert. Farms need to be irrigated in order for crops to grow. The only wild plants are those that need little water,

▲ *The low Black Mountains of Arizona.*

such as the creosote bush, mesquite, yucca, and cactus. Cactuses can store water for lengthy periods. Many kinds of cactus grow in southwestern Arizona. The largest—the saguaro—takes about 100 years to reach its full height of 50 feet (15 m).

History Indians probably lived in the region 20,000 years ago. About A.D. 100, the Hohokam Indians (ancestors of the Papago and Pima Indians) settled in the Gila River valley. They were pit dwellers who built extensive irrigation ditches for their fields. The Mogollon Indians settled in the east, the Anasazi in the north.

The Pueblo Indians, descendants of the Anasazi, built many-storied houses of sun-baked stone and clay. Many of these cliff dwellings, called *pueblos*, still stand. In the 1300's, the Apache and Navaho Indians moved into the region, and later the Hopi, Yuma, and other tribes came. The Indians lived mostly by farming, not hunting. Corn was their main food.

▲ *A view of Phoenix, state capital of Arizona.*

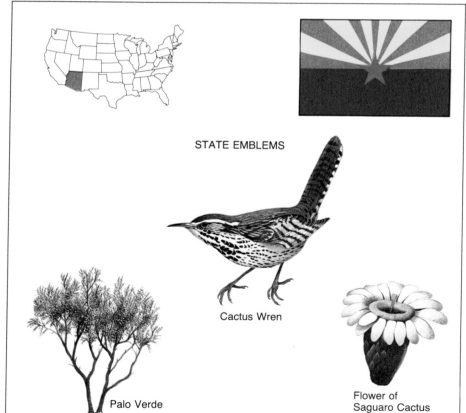

STATE EMBLEMS

Cactus Wren

Palo Verde

Flower of
Saguaro Cactus

ARIZONA

Capital and largest city
Phoenix (853,000 people)

Area
113,909 square miles
(295,023 sq. km)
Rank: 6th

Population
3,489,000 people
Rank: 25th

Statehood
February 14, 1912
(48th state admitted)

Principal river
Colorado River: 690 miles
(1,110 km) in Arizona

Highest point
Humphreys Peak: 12,633
feet (3,851 m)

Motto
Ditat Devs ("God Enriches")

Song
"Arizona"

Famous People
Cochise, Geronimo, Zane
Grey, Helen Jacobs, Barry
Goldwater, Frank Lloyd Wright

In the early 1500's Spaniards in New Spain (later known as Mexico) became interested in the country to the north. Estevanico, a black man, guided Marcos de Niza, a Spanish priest, to the Arizona area. In 1540, Marcos guided a Spanish expedition led by Francisco Coronado. The Spaniards explored a huge area. They made Arizona and much other land part of New Spain. Spanish priests later brought Christianity to the farming tribes of Indians.

Many Arizona Indians had a fierce love of freedom. They rebelled against white rule more than once. In 1821, Mexico (which included Arizona) won independence from Spain. Warlike northern Indians then became even bolder. After an uprising in 1827, whites gave up many settlements in Arizona. They moved farther south in Mexico, where they felt safer.

Arizona did not remain Mexican for long. The U.S. won a war with Mexico in 1848. Most of what is now the southwestern U.S., including Arizona, became part of U.S. territory through the peace treaty with Mexico in 1848 and the Gadsden Purchase in 1853.

American pioneers moved into Arizona. They took over land for farms and ranches. Indians sometimes attacked them. Cochise, Geronimo, and Mangus Coloradas led the Apaches in many raids against the whites. U.S. troops under General George Crook waged war against the Indians (1882–1885).

The Indians finally surrendered and agreed to live in special areas called *reservations*, which the Federal Government set aside for them. Even today Arizona has more than 174,000 Indians living on or near reservations. Seven in every hundred Arizona citizens are Indians.

Arizona became the 48th U.S. state in 1912. More and more people settled there to raise cattle, operate mines, or enjoy their retirement years.

Natural Resources Arizona's minerals include copper, gold, silver, lead, uranium ore, oil sands, and zinc. The state is especially rich in copper. More than one-half of all the copper mined in the United States comes from Arizona. Another natural resource is timber from the forests on Arizona's mountain slopes.

More land could be farmed if there were more water for irrigation. Arizona tries to make the best possible use of its limited supply of water. Much water falls in the Arizona mountains in the form of snow. The snow begins to melt in the spring. To catch the water, dams have been built across rivers. The mighty Boulder Dam was completed in 1936. The water backs up behind the dams and forms lakes. Canals and ditches take the water from the lakes to farms. Farmers also use water from underground wells that have not been pumped dry.

Arizonans at Work The leading industry of Arizona is making machinery, including airplane parts and electronic equipment. Mining is the second biggest business. Raising cattle and growing irrigated crops are also important. Cotton is the principal field crop in Arizona. But Arizona's third largest industry is not agriculture. It is tourism.

By far the most spectacular place to see is the Grand Canyon of the Colorado River. The canyon is actually a river valley carved out of the rock. It is more than 200 miles (320 km) long and from 4 to 18 miles (6 to 29 km) wide. It is a mile or more deep in some places. As sunlight changes during the day, the rocky walls change their colors. Two other unusual sights in Arizona are the Petrified Forest, made up of ancient tree trunks that have turned to stone, and the Painted Desert, with its strangely colored stone and sand. Other tourist attractions are the Lake Mead recreation area, the rebuilt London Bridge

▲ *Window Rock is a huge natural bridge in Arizona.*

When French explorers arrived in the area that is now the state of Arkansas they found an Indian tribe that called itself the Akansa or Akansea. The French spelled the name in various ways, but soon they settled on the spelling *Arkansas*. When the United States bought Arkansas in 1803 the Americans took over the French pronunciation of the name and they spelled it *Arkansaw*. That was the way it sounded. Finally, in 1881, the state legislature declared that the spelling was to be *Arkansas* but the name was to be pronounced ARK-un-saw.

at Lake Havasu City, and Meteor Crater.

ALSO READ: CORONADO, FRANCISCO; ESTEVANICO; EXPLORATION; GRAND CANYON; MEXICO; PAINTED DESERT; PETRIFIED FOREST.

ARKANSAS

The state of Arkansas was given the official nickname "The Land of Opportunity" in 1953. People have used the rich natural resources of the state to make a better life for themselves. Arkansas's businesses, factories, farms, and mines have thrived through people's effort.

Arkansas is a southern state. It lies near the center of the South. The broad, brown Mississippi River flows past the eastern edge of Arkansas. Missouri is north of Arkansas, Louisiana is south of it, and Oklahoma is to the west. Texas is at the southwest corner of Arkansas.

The Land Arkansas's land is partly high, partly low. Its highlands are in the northwest. The rest of the state is made up of low plains. The valley of the Arkansas River divides the highlands in two. The Boston Mountains, north of the river, are the roughest part of a big high area, the Ozark Plateau. A good place to see the Boston Mountains is at Devil's Den State Park. Huge, strangely shaped rocks can be seen in this park. The Boston Mountains are too steep to farm. They have been left mostly as forest land.

The Ouachita Mountains, south of

the Arkansas River, are also forested. The name "Ouachita" comes from an Indian word meaning "Good Hunting Grounds." Little Rock, the capital of Arkansas, is in the Ouachita foothills, low hills rising to the mountains. Westward, the Ouachita Mountains get higher. Some are over 2,500 feet (760 m).

Much good farmland lies in the Arkansas Valley. Farmers raise crops near the Arkansas River. The land is fairly level there, and the soil is better. Cattle graze where the hillsides are too steep for plowing and harvesting. The best Arkansas farmland is in the rolling plains of the lowlands. Most of the soil there is very fertile. The Ozark and Ouachita regions have usually silty and sandy soils.

Arkansas has an in-between climate. Winters are not cold. The average January temperature is 38°F (3°C). Summers are warm. The average temperature in July is 80°F (27°C). Winds blow mostly from the southwest, bringing warmth to Arkansas. Spring starts early and fine autumn weather lasts until December. The result is a long growing season. Plenty of rain falls throughout the year. Autumn, the time for harvesting crops, is the driest season.

Natural Resources Because Arkansas has many rivers, lakes, and springs, it has an abundant water supply that is convertible into hydroelectric power. The state's most important mineral resources are oil, bauxite, bromine, and natural gas. The state produces most of the nation's bauxite—the source of aluminum. Also, there is plenty of stone, gravel, and sand.

Forests cover almost three-fifths of the state. Oak, hickory, pine, ash, gum, and other trees are cut for lumber or wood products.

Arkansas is noted for its wild flowers, ferns, and herbs. There are American bellflowers, yellow jasmines, orchids, and water lilies.

▶ *An aerial view of the State Capitol at Little Rock, Arkansas.*

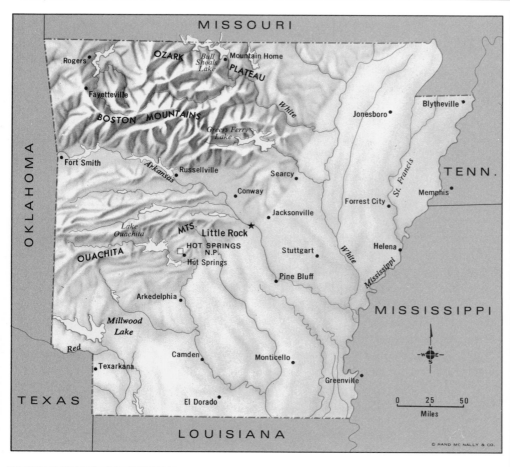

ARKANSAS

Capital and largest city
Little Rock
(170,000 people)

Area
53,104 square miles
(137,539 sq. km)
Rank: 27th

Population
2,395,000 people
Rank: 33rd

Statehood
June 15, 1836
(25th state admitted)

Principal river
Arkansas River:
250 miles (402 km)
in Arkansas

Highest point
Magazine Mountain:
2,823 feet (860 m)

Motto
Regnat Populus
("The People Rule")

Song
"Arkansas"

Famous People
Hattie Caraway,
James W. Fulbright,
Douglas MacArthur,
James S. McDonnel,
Winthrop Rockefeller

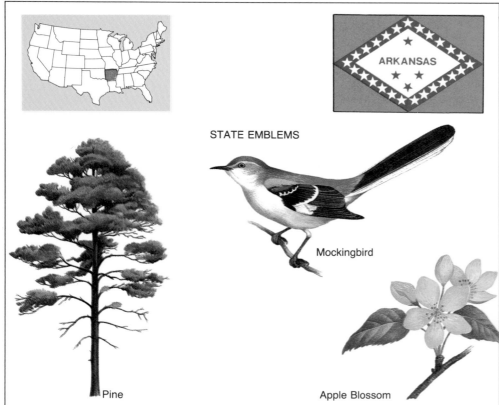

STATE EMBLEMS

Mockingbird

Pine

Apple Blossom

▲ *A 216-foot (65-m) high tower in Hot Springs.*

Wildlife is a natural resource. Among the animals in the state's forest are deer, bears, foxes, muskrats, minks, and many kinds of birds. Arkansas is on the Mississippi flyway, a broad north-south path along which millions of birds migrate each spring and fall. Eastern Arkansas is an important resting place for wild ducks and geese in the fall, when they are flying south.

History Spanish soldiers under Hernando de Soto were the first Europeans to enter what is now Arkansas. They came seeking gold in 1541 but did not settle. More than 100 years passed before Europeans again came to Arkansas. This time they were French explorers. The Indians whom the French met were northern people who had traveled south down the Mississippi River to reach this pleasant land. The Indians called themselves "Downstream People." The French never learned to say the Indian word for "Downstream People." "Arkansas" was as close as they could come.

What is now Arkansas became part of the huge Louisiana territory, claimed by France. The U.S. government bought the whole territory from France in 1803, for 15 million dollars. Arkansas became a state of the Union in 1836.

Arkansas had over 400,000 people by 1860. More than one-quarter of the population were black slaves. Arkansas joined other southern slave states in breaking away from the U.S. in 1861 and forming the Confederacy. The Confederate States were defeated in the Civil War, lasting from 1861 until 1865. All slaves were afterward freed.

Since the Civil War, Arkansas has had many struggling farmers. The constant planting of a single crop—cotton—wore out the soil in many areas. The average farmer lacked the money to buy the machinery, fertilizer, and other equipment needed for modern farming. Poverty and the Great Depression drove hundreds of families out of the state in the 1930's and 1940's.

Modern Arkansas at Work In 1955 Arkansas set up the Industrial Development Commission to try to bring in more industry. The Arkansas River Development Program improved navigation on the Arkansas River and built new water-power plants to supply cheap electricity and new flood control dams. Many new factories were attracted to the state. Thousands of new jobs became available. Today, over half of the state's people live in towns and cities.

Manufacturing earns more money for Arkansas than farming. Important products are foodstuffs, lumber, paper, and electrical machinery. Farming is still very important in the state. Soybeans are the crop which brings in the most money for farmers. Chickens, rice, cattle, and cotton are also grown.

Thousands of tourists visit Arkansas each year. Many of them go to Hot Springs National Park to swim, boat, fish, and camp. Some people find that bathing in the water from the hot springs improves their health. Visitors can hunt for diamonds in the only diamond mine in the United States, located near Murfreesboro. Other attractions for visitors vacationing in the state include Blanchard Caverns, Eureka Springs, and Dogpatch U.S.A.

ALSO READ: CIVIL WAR, LOUISIANA PURCHASE, MISSISSIPPI RIVER, RECONSTRUCTION.

ARMADILLO Strange defenses have helped certain animal species survive. The armadillo's armorlike covering is its protection. The armadillo is a long-tongued mammal whose chief food is insects. It is fairly small but heavy. The name "armadillo'' means "little armored one" in Spanish.

An armadillo is born with a soft, leathery covering. The special skin of armor plates or bands hardens, except at the joints, as the animal grows. The armor coat may cover the legs and tail. Armadillos are timid creatures and burrow quickly to hide when they are attacked. The armadillo's armor sticks up above ground to plug up its burrow. The *three-banded armadillo* can roll up completely in a hard ball.

About 20 different species of armadillo live in South and Central America. The smallest is the *fairy armadillo*, a tiny pink animal. The largest is the *giant armadillo*. It grows up to 4 feet (1.2 m) long. The *nine-banded armadillo* of Mexico and the southwestern United States spends sunny days in its burrow. It hunts insects and snakes at night. This armadillo has the amazing ability to swallow air so its intestines inflate. It can then float across a river like a rubber raft.

ALSO READ: ANTEATER, MAMMAL, SKIN, SLOTH.

▲ *The armadillo has a coat of scaly armor for defense. It can also burrow quickly to escape its enemies.*

ARMOR In ancient times, soldiers fought with swords, spears, knives, and bows and arrows. Most battles were fought hand-to-hand. Soldiers needed protection that they could wear or carry. The items a soldier wore or carried to shield his body from wounds were known as *armor*.

The earliest armor may have been coats made of layers of heavily quilted cloth. Ancient Egyptians and Assyrians wore this kind of armor as early as 3000 B.C. Homer, the Greek poet, described armor made of leather and bronze, worn during the Trojan War.

Armor often had three main parts—helmet, jacket, and leg-coverings. A metal helmet was worn to protect the soldier's head. The helmet had a chin strap so it would not fall off. There were two types of jackets,

both of which came down to the knees. A jacket made of *chain mail* had many small rings of metal hooked closely together, like a knitted sweater. Chain mail was used in Europe 2,000 years ago. It was light and flexible, so the wearer could move easily. The second type of jacket was made of leather or padded cloth with overlapping strips of metal sewn to it. This plate-type material was stronger than chain mail, but heavier. It was developed by ancient Egyptians and Persians. Both types were popular as long as armor was used. Soldiers often wore both kinds of jackets, one over the other. *Greaves* were pieces of

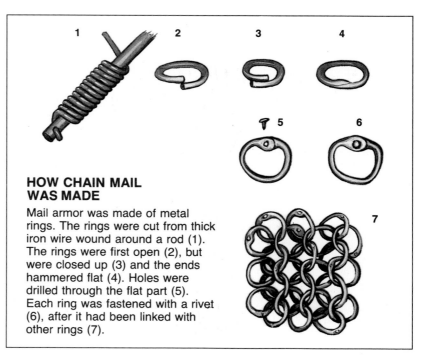

HOW CHAIN MAIL WAS MADE

Mail armor was made of metal rings. The rings were cut from thick iron wire wound around a rod (1). The rings were first open (2), but were closed up (3) and the ends hammered flat (4). Holes were drilled through the flat part (5). Each ring was fastened with a rivet (6), after it had been linked with other rings (7).

leather or metal that strapped around the soldier's leg below the knee.

Soldiers also carried shields. The first shields were probably made of wood covered with leather. Later shields were made of metal. A shield had a strap on the inside that fitted over the soldier's arm. It also had a hand grip so he could hold it firmly. The best shields were thick enough to protect a soldier, but light enough to be carried in battle.

Knights in Armor In the late part of the Middle Ages, from about the 1400's to the 1500's, Europeans used another kind of armor called *Gothic* armor. This armor was a metal suit that covered the whole body, except for small slits in the helmet. Even the gloves were made of armor. Each suit had to be especially made for the person who wore it. Gothic armor was worn in battle mainly by knights. Their horses often wore metal armor, too.

A knight's main weapon was a *lance*, a long, sharp, heavy spear that fitted into a holder on the armor and rested on the saddle. He charged with his lance pointed at enemy knights. Of course, the other knights had lances too. Other weapons used by knights were swords, hammers, flails, and clubs. Armored warriors carried

▼ *Examples of styles of armor. Each part of a suit of plate armor had a special name.*

1 visor	5 cuisse
2 breastplate	6 greave
3 gauntlet	7 sabaton
4 couter	

Norman, around 1100

Saracen, around 1200

Crusader, around 1200

Plate armor, around 1500

13th-century helmet

Keay

heavy metal shields to defend themselves. If a knight were knocked off his horse, the armor was so heavy that he had a hard time getting up again. One rule of battle was that a knight could be captured while lying on the ground, but he had to be well treated as a prisoner.

Full suits of armor were made for knights with horses, but lighter models were also made for foot soldiers. Owners of suits of armor paid much money for them. Some armor had beautiful designs and jewels.

Friendly knights fought each other in sporting contests in times of peace. They entertained crowds and kept in practice for war. These contests were called *jousts*, or tournaments. At the jousts, knights wore extra heavy armor and used lances without points. The knight who knocked the other off his horse won.

In the early 1500's, guns made suits of armor uselessly out of date. Bullets could pass through armor, and in a gun fight, armor was too heavy anyway. However, armor is still used today. Soldiers and police officers on riot patrol often wear helmets and bulletproof vests made of steel plates sewn to cloth. Construction workers and fire fighters wear *hard hats* to protect them from falling objects. In sports, race car drivers, motorcyclists, football players, hockey players, polo players, and baseball umpires wear various kinds of armor to keep them from getting hurt badly.

Armored Vehicles. From the 1800's warships were strengthened with steel armor plate to protect them against gunfire. During World War I armored cars and tanks made their first appearance on the battlefield. During World War II airplanes, too, were armored.

Today, civil armored cars are used to transport gold, money, and payrolls. They are designed to withstand attack by criminals, and are protection against gunfire and poison gas.

ARMSTRONG, LOUIS (1900–1971)

Louis Armstrong was a showman as well as a great jazz musician. His many concerts in Europe were such triumphs that he was called one of America's most popular goodwill ambassadors.

Armstrong was born in New Orleans, Louisiana. He learned to play trumpet in an orphans' home in that city. As the music called jazz developed, Louis Armstrong, nicknamed "Satchmo," helped it grow. In 1922, he went to Chicago. There he won fame in King Oliver's band. Armstrong started his own band in 1925. He played his horn freely and wildly, often improvising, inventing new melodies as he played. Sometimes he used his gravelly voice to shout meaningless sounds to the music—a style called *scat singing*.

Louis Armstrong's trumpet improvisation became the envy of other jazz musicians. Armstrong went to New York in 1929, where he led many bands. He made many records, including some of his own jazz compositions. Appearances in films and television, and at jazz festivals, made him known all over the world. In 1966, he won an award for best jazz musician at the First World Festival of Negro Arts, in Dakar, Senegal. He told the story of his start in jazz in his autobiography, *Satchmo: My Life in New Orleans.*

ALSO READ: BRASS INSTRUMENTS, JAZZ.

Some armor was immensely heavy. That worn by Charles V of Spain, together with his horse's armor, weighed no less than 220 pounds (100 kg), much more than Charles himself. It is preserved in the Royal Armory in Madrid.

The thickest armor ever used was on the British battleship *Inflexible*, built in 1881. It was 24 inches (61 cm) thick. Behind it were teak planks, giving a total thickness of 42 inches (107 cm).

◀ *Louis Armstrong, jazz musician and entertainer.*

ARMSTRONG, NEIL (born 1930)
"That's one small step for a man, one giant leap for mankind." With those words, Neil Armstrong climbed from the Apollo lunar module *Eagle* and became the first man to stand on the moon, on July 20, 1969. This was the high point of his flying career, which began when he was 16.

Neil Armstrong was born in Wapakoneta, Ohio. He earned his Navy wings at 19. He flew 78 missions in the Korean War. As a test pilot, he flew an X-15 rocket plane to 207,000 feet (63 km) at 3,818 miles an hour (6,144 km/hr).

The National Aeronautics and Space Administration (NASA) picked Armstrong and eight others to be astronauts in September 1962. In March 1966, after almost four years of training, Armstrong and David Scott flew Gemini 8 and performed the first successful docking of two vehicles in space. Armstrong's next mission was as commander of the Apollo 11 moonlanding.

One year after the Apollo 11 flight with Edwin Aldrin and Michael Collins, Armstrong went to work with NASA in Washington, D.C.

ALSO READ: ALDRIN, EDWIN; ASTRONAUT; COLLINS, MICHAEL; MOON; SPACE TRAVEL.

The oldest army in the world is the colorfully dressed Swiss Guard in Vatican City. The origins of this guard go back to before 1400.

▶ *Neil Armstrong, first person on the moon.*

ARMY An army is an organized group of soldiers who are trained to fight mostly on land. During a war, the main job of an army is to defend the homeland or to invade and gain control of enemy territory and the enemy army. Even after a war is over, an army may stay and control the territory it has conquered.

Ancient Armies People have always fought one another, but they have not always had professional armies. The earliest wars were short battles between tribes, usually over a piece of land that both tribes wanted. Every man who was able and willing to fight picked up a club and some stones and joined the battle. After the battle was over, the men returned to their everyday lives. The first professional armies developed with the growth of great civilizations in the Middle East, Egypt, and China. The soldiers of a professional army are paid to be in the army full-time, whether a war is on or not. When there is no war, they practice using their weapons and study techniques of warfare.

Ancient armies were first made up of *infantry*, or soldiers who fight on foot. The Assyrians are thought to have been the first to use horses in battle. They had charioteers and *cavalry*, or soldiers who fight on horseback. Today, the name "cavalry" is sometimes used for soldiers who operate tanks and armored cars, and even for airborne fighters.

In the city-states of ancient Greece every young man had to serve in the army for a time. This practice is known as *universal service*. In Sparta, boys began their military training at the age of seven. They continued to serve in the army until they were 60. Compulsory service in the army existed in ancient Persia and Rome and in Europe during the Middle Ages. France adopted the modern military *draft* system, or *conscription*, in 1792. Napoleon formed huge French armies from *draftees*. Today, most nations in time of war use the draft to raise armies. Some nations, like Israel, draft men and women.

An army is usually made up of soldiers who fight for their own nation. But sometimes a nation hires foreign soldiers called *mercenaries*. They promise to be loyal to the nation that hires them. Probably the most famous mercenary army of all times was the French Foreign Legion, started in 1831. It fought for France all over the world.

What Makes a Good Soldier Six important things make soldiers fight well—strong leaders, efficient weapons, adequate supply lines, good training, firm discipline, and high morale.

The leaders must know how to plan and fight wars well so the soldiers will trust their orders, even in times of great danger. The weapons must be at least good enough to give the soldier a fair chance in fighting the enemy. Many modern weapons are very complicated, and the soldiers must be carefully trained to use them properly.

▶ *Persian armies had cavalry and infantry. Soldiers sometimes rode war elephants into battle.*

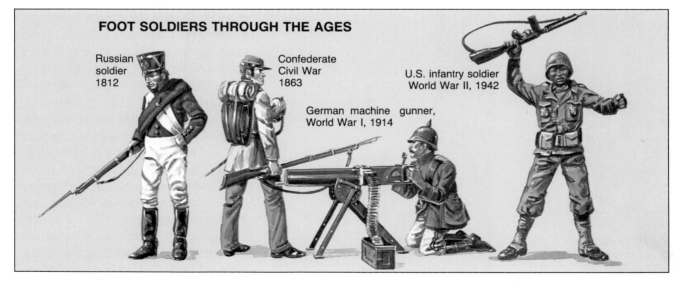

FOOT SOLDIERS THROUGH THE AGES

Russian soldier 1812

Confederate Civil War 1863

German machine gunner, World War I, 1914

U.S. infantry soldier World War II, 1942

▶ *Soldiers of the French Foreign Legion march down a street in Djibouti, once part of France's colonial empire in Africa.*

▲ *A soldier uses a field radio to keep in touch with other units in the battle area.*

Discipline makes a soldier obey orders and keep fighting, even when he is tired, frightened, or does not understand fully the reasons for the orders. It comes from good training and inspiring leadership.

High morale or *esprit de corps* often makes the difference between winning or losing. *Esprit de corps* means the soldier has confidence in his leaders, himself, and the other people on his side. It means pride, too, and belief in a cause. In the American Revolution, the Continental Army held together in the terrible cold winter at Valley Forge because of high morale.

▶ *A soldier learns how to cross a river on a simple bridge made of a single rope. Basic training is a vital part of the modern army.*

The U.S. Army Before the American Revolution, each colony had a *militia* made up of men of all ages who were prepared to fight if needed. Militiamen made up the backbone of the Continental Army when it was formed in 1775 under the leadership of George Washington. One command, or branch, of the Army is still called the Continental Army. It is in charge of the ground defense of the United States. Other combat commands are stationed in the Atlantic, the Pacific, Europe, South Korea, and Alaska. Some commands are joint operations with other services. For example, the Army and the Air Force work together in the Tactical Air Command.

The men of the Army are volunteers. After passing certain health requirements, they go through basic training to learn about the Army, their weapons, and simple field activities. They then go into special training for combat with helicopters, tanks, or missiles, for example, or for support work. The support troops include people who work with supplies, communications, research, or the business of running the Army. Some men learn to be officers, or leaders of men.

The U.S. Army has a women's branch called the Women's Army Corps (WAC). The women are volunteers also. They do not serve in combat but provide much support that releases men for more hazardous jobs. Women also serve as nurses and medical workers.

The reserves and the National Guard back up the regular U.S. Army. Reserves are men and women who train for a short time every year, so that they are ready for active duty in case of war. Each state organizes its own National Guard, which is controlled by the governor. The reserves and the National Guard are called into the regular army to fight only by order of the President with the approval of Congress.

Armies today have other important jobs besides fighting wars. One is riot control. A riot happens when a crowd of people becomes violent. Sometimes a riot is so big that the local police cannot stop it. The army is ordered to help. Another job of an

▼ A soldier of a United Nations peacekeeping force on patrol. Soldiers from many nations may serve in such a U.N. force. But the U.N. has no permanent army of its own.

army is to help people in case of natural disasters such as floods, hurricanes, forest fires, and earthquakes. Armies have often been called on to help build roads and dams, to dredge rivers, or to aid in health projects, such as malaria control.

ALSO READ: AIR FORCE; ARMOR; EISENHOWER, DWIGHT D.; FORTIFICATION; GUERRILLA WARFARE; GUNS AND RIFLES; MACARTHUR, DOUGLAS; MILITARY ACADEMY; NATIONAL GUARD; TANK; WEAPONS.

ARNOLD, BENEDICT see ALLEN, ETHAN; TREASON.

ART Who can say what art is? Or even what good art is? Surely art is doing, making, creating something of your own. It gives you a good feeling inside that you have done something new and exciting. Art can take many forms. It can be writing a story or playing a song on the piano that sounded just right. It can be making a finger painting that is bright and swirly. It can be digging deep into a blob of clay and bringing about a pleasant shape. Art for you might be dancing out a story you made up. It could be acting out a fairy tale with some friends or reading a special poem out loud to people who care. What is art for you? It must be something you like to do that satisfies you.

Art of Different Times and Places
New arts spring up everywhere. All peoples of the world have developed some art forms. Many children who live in the country come to know birds very well and have often learned to make beautiful bird calls. That is a kind of art. Others draw and paint pictures of the birds they see. This art is better known. In the mountains of Switzerland many years ago, people made many kinds of bells. That finally led to the art of the Swiss bell

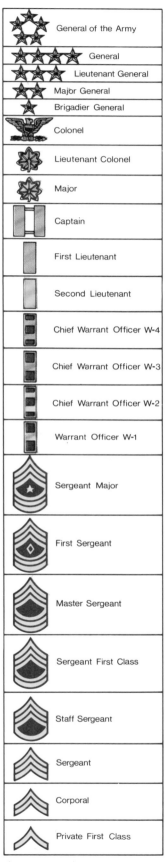

▲ Insignia of rank in the U. S. Army.

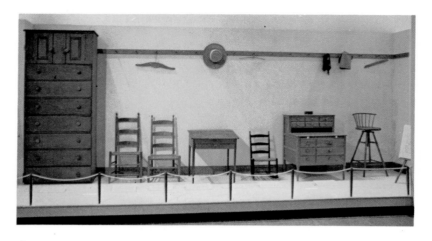

▲ *Good art is pleasing to look at and can be useful too. The Shakers were a religious group who made beautiful furniture.*

The largest art gallery in the world is the Winter Palace and Hermitage in Leningrad, U.S.S.R. There are nearly 3 million works of art and you would have to walk about 15 miles (24 km) to see them all.

ringer. Maybe you can make up your own new art!

Some children take part in art at the professional level. The Vienna Choir Boys, for example, travel about the world giving concerts. They sing beautiful music by the greatest composers and perform for thousands of people. The oldest boys in the choir are 13 or 14. The youngest are about 8 or 9.

Children from many parts of the world who like to paint have had their paintings shown in the international exhibits sponsored by the United Nations Educational, Scientific, and Cultural Organization (UNESCO) at the U.N. in New York and in many foreign lands.

Sometimes, talent for a certain art runs through a family. There are families who enjoy singing together. Michael Jackson and his brothers sang together for some years. Other families have all played musical instruments and have had family orchestras. Some families, like the Wyeths, have several painters in them. The Booth and Barrymore families had a number of actors and actresses.

You may develop an art any time in your life. In 1961 an old woman died in New York State at age 101 years. She was called "Grandma Moses" (Anna Mary Robertson Moses). She was a hard-working woman who reared a large family and kept a big farm going until she was old. She did

sewing and embroidery. But her hands became stiff with arthritis, and she couldn't sew anymore. Then someone gave her a box of paints. She began painting pictures of life on the farm in the olden days. People liked her pictures and began to buy them. By the time she was in her eighties, she was famous. Before she died she had lived a new life with the art she had found in her old age.

Some forms of art are not always well accepted when they are first introduced. But later they come to be highly prized. This was true of the French Impressionists of the late 1800's. People laughed at these young artists' paintings and wouldn't let them into exhibitions. Now the Impressionists' work is highly prized. Pierre Auguste Renoir (1841–1919) was a French Impressionist. It is hard to realize that *A Girl with a Watering Can* was not liked when it was first painted!

Some talented artists are not discovered until after they die. The poet Emily Dickinson is very famous now, but no one in her home town of Amherst, Massachusetts, thought of shy Emily in the white dress as a poet. After she died, hundreds of poems in her handwriting were found in her dresser drawers, though she had only six poems printed when she was alive. She wrote poetry all her life, not to get attention from the world, but because she loved creating poetry.

Art Among Groups Groups of people sometimes produce certain kinds of art. One talent seems to spark another. An unusual religious group called the *Shakers* lived more than 200 years ago in a community in New York State. Some of the craftsmen in this group made beautiful furniture. Their designs were handsome and the woodworking was very well done. Today Shakers have all but disappeared. But Shaker furniture is prized in museums as beautiful art. Who were the Shaker carpenters? No one knows their names, but working together they made furniture that is lasting art.

In the days of slavery in the South, blacks created the art of the *spiritual*—a song of worship that is great American music, songs like "Swing Low, Sweet Chariot" and "Little David, Play on Your Harp." Why did spirituals develop? Who wrote them? No one can say. Slaves were forbidden by law to read and write. They had little chance to learn to play musical instruments. But nothing could stop them from singing. They sang as they picked cotton, lifted heavy loads, and did a thousand hard chores in the hot sun. And they created an art—making up songs, the words and music of which they could not even write down. It was a great art, from an unexpected place.

Fine Arts and Applied Arts In our times, arts that are intended just for beauty are called *fine arts*. These include sculpture, painting, music, dance, drawing, literature, architecture, and drama. Which one is your favorite now? You might enjoy trying every one of the fine arts at some time in your life.

The principles of design and

▲ A Girl with a Watering Can *by the Impressionist painter Auguste Renoir. National Gallery of Art, Washington, D.C., Chester Dale Collection.*

◄ Hoosick Falls in Winter. *The paintings of Grandma Moses are of happy and carefree days in the countryside. She did not begin painting until she was 76.*

229

The biggest "old master" painting is in the Doge's Palace in Venice, Italy. It is *Il Paradiso* by Tintoretto and measures 72 feet 2 inches by 22 feet 11½ inches (22 m by 7 m). There are 350 people in the picture.

The most valuable painting in the world is thought to be the *Mona Lisa* by Leonardo de Vinci, which hangs in the Louvre in Paris. It is quite small—only 30½ by 21 inches (77 by 53 cm), and it is said that King Francis I of France once had it hanging in his bedroom.

▼ *A wood carving of a reclining figure, by the British sculptor Henry Moore (1898–1986).*

beauty in the fine arts are put to use in the *applied arts*. People now feel that everything that is built or made in a factory should be done with good design. This is *everyday art*. Lovers of everyday art say that the bridge you cross on your way to school should be beautiful to look at. The school that you walk into every morning should be pleasing to the eye. Your desk there should be made graceful as well as comfortable. The dishes in your school cafeteria should be pretty to look at, besides being big enough to hold your hot lunch. Everyday art goes further—*to beautification*. Why should you pass an ugly dump of wrecked automobiles on your way to school? That dump can be cleaned up, and trees planted there. Beauty can grow by the roadside for you to enjoy every day.

In the future, you may work at jobs only three or four days a week. Machines will help people do some of their work. You will have more free time than any people in history. You will have more time for the arts. Very often the arts you like as a child become the arts you love as a grown-up. What arts would you choose as hobbies? The important thing is that you enjoy them. Your art should say, "This is *me*. This is what *I* think." And only you can say what arts are for you.

ALSO READ: ARCHITECTURE, ART HISTORY, DANCE, DRAMA, DRAWING, LITERATURE, MUSIC, PAINTING, SCULPTURE.

ART HISTORY People throughout history have loved drawing, painting, sculpture, and other visual arts. In fact, some people say that the most important test of a civilization is the art it produces. Many civilizations that have vanished completely are known only for their beautiful art. Art often recorded events of a culture.

The most ancient art was done by the people of the Old Stone Age. Their art has been found in caves in France and Spain and several places in Africa. Look at the painting of a bison. It was found deep in a cave at Altamira, Spain. See what bright colors the artist used, earth colors made from different colors of soil. The artist carried the paints deep into the cave and, working by torchlight, painted this picture of a dying bison on the wall. The bison has long since disappeared from Spain. We know almost nothing of the people who painted the picture, exactly when they lived, or what they thought. Yet, we can look at this picture now, about 30,000 years after it was painted, and be thrilled with its color and life and the story it tells us.

Ancient Art Thousands of years passed between the time of the cave paintings and the dawn of *recorded time*—after written language had been

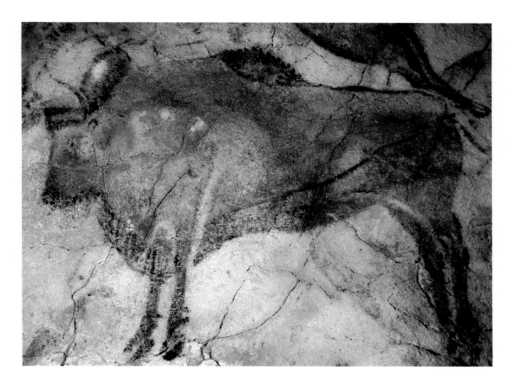

invented. The Egyptians were among the earliest people to use written language. They built a remarkable civilization beside the Nile River. Most of their art history has been found in their famous pyramids, built as tombs for their rulers. The Egyptian rulers spent years getting ready for their deaths. Their tombs were decorated with art to accompany them on their journey into the next world.

At the same time, the Chinese were producing beautiful art of the Bronze Age. Handsome bronze vessels made during the Chou Dynasty (the family of rulers from about 1766–1122 B.C.) are some outstanding examples of ancient art. Chinese artists produced great work for the next 2,000 years.

A few hundred years later (600–100 B.C.) Indian tribes in Middle America made beautiful sculpture. The statue of a woman from ancient Mexico (see picture) reveals the human figure without copying its details. Notice her lively expression.

The greatest culture of the ancient world was in its glory in the years from 460 to 300 B.C. The Greeks were perhaps the most artistic people in world history. They designed beauti-

ful buildings. They had long since mastered the working of bronze. They also made clay pottery of great perfection. Their bronze and marble sculpture had a longer period of greatness. The marble statue (see picture on next page) of Hermes, the messenger god, is by Praxiteles, a great Greek sculptor who lived from about 390 to 330 B.C. Hermes is holding the infant god Bacchus. The statue has beautiful curves, and the figure is standing in a relaxed manner.

Christianity changed the lives of people, as it spread in the first few hundred years after Christ. Religion became the subject of most art. The painting of Christ (see picture on next page) is by an unknown artist of the late days of the Roman Empire, about A.D. 600. It shows Christ as a young man, in the way the people of the early church saw him.

Compare this picture of Christ with a painting of baby Jesus and Mary done several hundred years later. The artist, Giotto di Bondone (about 1276–1337), was born near Florence, Italy. He decorated the little Arena Chapel in Padua, starting in 1304. The painting on the next page is from

▼ *A statue of a woman from ancient Mexico.*

ART HISTORY

▶ Christ Enthroned *by an unknown artist about* A.D. *600.*

▼ Hermes *by Praxiteles, the Greek sculptor.*

the chapel. See how he arranged a few solid-looking forms in space? Note how different his style was from the flat style of the earlier painting. Giotto made a great breakthrough in painting. He developed depth.

The Renaissance Giotto and his glorious work came at the beginning of a very exciting time in European painting—the Renaissance. The word means "rebirth." The rebirth of the arts was brought about by a renewed interest in ancient arts. Painting and sculpture were encouraged as Florence, Venice, and other Italian cities became wealthy from world trade. An amazing number of talented artists lived and worked within a period of 200 years or so. Three of the greatest—the masters of the High Renaissance in Italy—were Leonardo da Vinci (1452–1519), Michelangelo Buonarroti (1475–1564), and Raphael (1483–1520).

Michelangelo was a sculptor and painter. One of his greatest projects was painting scenes from the Old Testament on the ceiling of the Sistine Chapel at the Vatican in Rome. The ceiling is 118 feet (36 m) long. The painting of God creating Adam (see picture) is one of the most famous parts of the ceiling. Michelangelo painted the picture of Adam in three days. It is 13 feet (4 m) high. The whole project took four years.

The Renaissance spread, and much of Europe came alive with a rebirth of art and culture. Many Renaissance paintings, particularly in the Netherlands, were concerned with everyday events in the lives of people. Frans Hals (1580–1666), Rembrandt van Rijn (1606–1669), and Jan Vermeer (1632–1675) were the three greatest Dutch painters. Vermeer liked to paint pictures of women with light coming from one window. He usually chose one small subject and painted with great perfection. *The Lace Maker* (see picture) is a good example. See how the yellow dress of the pretty woman seems to give a glow to the light on her face.

In the 1700's Britain became a rich country. With wealth came the encouragement of art. Portrait painting was particularly important. Such artists as Sir Joshua Reynolds (1723–1792) and Thomas Gainsborough (1727–1788) were very much in demand for portraits of important people. John Constable (1776–1837) and J. M. W. Turner (1775–1851) were fine painters of landscapes. In Germany, Caspar David Friedrich (1774–1840) made landscape painting a form of religious art.

▼ The Birth of Jesus *by Giotto.*

▲ The Creation of Adam *by Michelangelo, painted on the ceiling of the Sistine Chapel in Rome, Italy. The artist took four years to complete the task.*

▲ The Lace Maker *by Jan Vermeer.*

▲ Two Men Contemplating the Moon *by Caspar David Friedrich. Painted in 1819, it is a fine example of German Romantic art.*

▲ *John Hoyland's* Acrylic on Canvas *is an example of contemporary abstract art. The viewer can make up his or her own mind about the subject.*

ART AROUND THE WORLD

	AFRICA	THE AMERICAS	ASIA	EUROPE
Today	Modern African	Modern American Pop Art Mexican Muralists	Modern Asian Cubism	Modern European Surrealism Cubism Expressionism Post-Impressionism
		Hudson River School Colonial American Navaho	Edo Period in Japan	Impressionism Realism Romanticism
A.D. 1600	Benin		Mughal Dynasty in India	Rococo Baroque
	Ife Yoruba Ashanti Poro Baluba	Inca in Peru Aztec in Mexico	Ming Dynasty in China	Renaissance Mannerism
		Pueblo	Sung Dynasty in China	
A.D. 1200	Zimbabwe			Gothic
		Toltec in Mexico	Islamic Tajng Dynasty in China	
		Classic Maya in Guatemala, Honduras, and Yucatán (Mexico)		Romanesque
A.D. 800			Oceanic in Pacific Islands	
			Gupta Period in India	Byzantine
		Teotihuacán in Mexico		
		Mochica in Peru	Six Dynasties in China	
			Nara Period in Japan	
A.D. 400				Early Christian
			Andhra Period in India	
	Nok		Han Dynasty in China	
A.D. B.C.				Roman Period
			Chou Period in China	
				Golden Age of Greece
400 B.C.		Pre-Classic Maya in Guatemala		
	Early Nok Kush			
		Andean		Etruscan Early Greek Period
800 B.C.		(South America)		
1200 B.C.	Egyptian Later Kingdom			Minoan (Crete)
			Shang Period in China	

The center of European art moved over to France in the late 1800's. The modern period of art began there when the Impressionists, a group of young artists in Paris, began painting. They wanted to work in the open air, away from the usual studio kind of art. They had an urge to paint the pure colors of nature, as in the paintings of Claude Monet (1840–1926), leader of the Impressionists of France. Most Impressionists were French.

The Impressionists began a new freedom in art that continued to grow. Since then, very many artists have experimented with new ways of painting. The Cubists, led by Pablo Picasso (1881–1973), were interested in abstract forms. But Picasso, unlike most painters, did not develop one style of painting. He would paint one way for a few years, then change his style completely.

Many new art styles developed in the United States after World War II. New York City is thought by many to be the world center of art, as Paris was for many hundreds of years. Among U.S. painters are Jackson Pollock (1912–1956), Mark Rothko (1930–1970), and Roy Lichtenstein (born 1923).

For further information on:
Kinds of Art, *see* ABSTRACT ART, ARCHITECTURE, CARVING, CLAY MODELING, DESIGN, DRAWING, ETCHING AND ENGRAVING, FOLK ART, GRAPHIC ARTS, MOSAIC, PAINTING, PAPER SCULPTURE, SCULPTURE, SYMBOLISM.
Arts of Many Peoples, *see* DUTCH ART, GREEK ART, INDIAN ART, MAYA, ORIENTAL ART, ROMAN ART.
Art Collections, *see* ART MUSEUMS AND GALLERIES, FLORENCE, LOUVRE, VATICAN CITY, VENICE.
Periods of Art, *see* BAROQUE PERIOD, IMPRESSIONISM, MODERN ART, RENAISSANCE, ROCOCO ART, ROMANESQUE ART, ROMANTIC PERIOD.
For individual artists see names in the Index volume.

ARTHROPOD see CENTIPEDES AND MILLIPEDES, CRUSTACEAN, INSECT, SPIDER.

ARTHUR, CHESTER A. (1830–1886) After President James A. Garfield was shot on July 2, 1881, there was much talk about what would happen if Vice President Chester A. Arthur became the President of the United States. Dishonesty in government was widespread at that time. People thought Arthur would give jobs to his friends and open the White House to loafers. But he became somewhat of a reformer.

He was born in Vermont, son of a Baptist minister. After Arthur graduated from Union College, he taught school in Vermont and later became a school principal in New York. He studied law and became a successful lawyer in New York City. Before the Civil War, he won fame defending the civil liberties of runaway slaves.

In 1860, Arthur helped Edwin D. Morgan win reelection as Republican governor of New York and was rewarded with the job of engineer-in-chief of the state. He reorganized the New York militia. Later President Ulysses S. Grant appointed him collector of the port of New York, a well-paid, powerful political position.

He was part of Roscoe Conkling's New York Republican machine. Though Arthur was removed by President Rutherford B. Hayes, he was given the Republican vice-presidential nomination through Conkling's help. He was elected with Garfield in 1880.

After Garfield died on September 19, 1881, Arthur became the 21st President of the United States. Many Americans thought Arthur was a man who would do whatever the Republican Party wanted. The Republican Party bosses thought so, too. But everyone was wrong. Arthur tried hard to do what he thought was right for the whole country, not just for the Republicans. He changed the *spoils system*, the practice of giving the best government jobs to the faithful supporters of the party. He also set up a merit system which gave the best jobs to those passing difficult examinations.

Arthur made other changes, too. He reorganized and modernized the U.S. Navy. He removed dishonest men who controlled the Post Office. He worked to admit Chinese immigrants to the U.S. He called an international conference for the purpose of establishing standard time zones around the globe.

The Republican Party leaders were angry with Arthur because he did not

Before Chester Arthur moved into the White House he thought it looked like "a badly kept barracks." He ordered it to be completely redecorated. New plumbing was installed, a new bathroom was added, and the first elevator was installed in the White House.

CHESTER A. ARTHUR
TWENTY-FIRST PRESIDENT   SEPTEMBER 20, 1881–MARCH 4, 1885

Born: October 5, 1830, Fairfield, Vermont
Parents: Reverend William and Malvina Stone Arthur
Education: Union College
Religion: Episcopalian
Occupation: Teacher and Lawyer
Political Party: Republican
Married: 1859 to Ellen Lewis Herndon (1837–1880)
Children: 2 sons (1 died in infancy), 1 daughter
Died: November 18, 1886, New York City
Buried: Albany, New York

In the 15th century an Englishman called Sir Thomas Malory gathered together many of the stories about King Arthur. They appeared in a book called *Morte d'Arthur* (Death of Arthur). This book was one of the very first books printed in English by William Caxton in 1485.

follow their orders. They did not nominate him for President again in 1884. But, when he retired to his New York home after four years as President, Arthur had won the respect of the nation.

ALSO READ: ASSASSINATION; GARFIELD, JAMES A.; GOVERNMENT CAREER; PRESIDENCY.

ARTHUR, KING Many old legends tell of Arthur, a strong war leader of the Celts, the people who lived in Britain 1,500 years ago, before the Saxons invaded the land in the 500's. The legends say that the country had no king for a short time in the 500's. The people prayed for help in choosing one. Suddenly a stone appeared outside a church. In the stone was stuck a mighty sword. Men from all over the land tried to pull the sword from the stone, but all failed. One day Arthur, the young son of the dead king, came forward and freed the sword. He was named king.

King Arthur was given another sword, called Excalibur, by the Lady of the Lake. He ruled with his beautiful queen, Guinevere. Their castle was Tintagel, according to some legends, or Camelot, according to others. Towns all over England, Scotland, and Wales still claim to have been the site of Arthur's castle. Arthur's faithful friend and adviser was Merlin, a poet, prophet, and magician. Arthur's knights helped bring peace to the country. They met with him around the famous Round Table, where all were considered equal.

Stories also tell that King Arthur's knights did wonderful deeds. But one of them, Sir Modred, was a traitor. He tried to become king. Arthur killed Modred in battle, but Arthur himself was wounded. King Arthur was carried off on a magic barge to the mysterious Isle of Avalon to be healed. According to the legend, one day Arthur will return to be king again.

Nothing is known about the real Arthur—if he existed. But the tales about Arthur, Merlin, and the Knights of the Round Table have become part of European culture and have fascinated people all over the world for centuries. Many of the world's best poets and musicians have written about this legendary hero.

ALSO READ: ENGLISH HISTORY, KNIGHTHOOD, LEGEND.

▶ *King Arthur and his knights of the Round Table.*

ARTICLE see PARTS OF SPEECH.

ARTICLES OF CONFEDERATION The 13 American colonies needed some system of rules to govern themselves after the Declaration of Independence was adopted on July 4, 1776. The agreement that set up the first United States Government was called the Articles of Confederation.

Under the Articles, each state kept its rights but granted some powers to the Continental Congress, called the "Congress of the Confederation." Congress had power over foreign affairs, disputes among states, national defense, money, Indian affairs, and states' claims to western territory.

All states had ratified (accepted) the Articles of Confederation by 1781. But people soon discovered that the Articles did not give the U.S. Government enough power to run the country. Congress could only *ask* the states for money but could not tax them. Congress had no control over trade among states or with foreign countries. The country had no president, king, or even federal judges.

It became clear that the Articles were not working very well. It was difficult to obtain the nine votes needed from the 13 states to pass any important measure. For a few years Congress struggled on, but eventually 55 delegates assembled at Philadelphia to revise the Articles. The Constitutional Convention met in May, 1787. The delegates wrote a whole new document instead—the Constitution of the United States. The Constitution went into effect on March 4, 1789, and is still the basic law of the United States.

ALSO READ: AMERICAN REVOLUTION; CONSTITUTION, UNITED STATES; CONTINENTAL CONGRESS; DECLARATION OF INDEPENDENCE.

ARTIFICIAL RESPIRATION

Anyone who stops breathing will usually die in four to six minutes. Drowning, electric shock, gas poisoning, misuse of drugs, or other causes can stop a person's breathing. Artificial respiration, done the right way, may save a life.

Mouth-to-mouth breathing is one way to make a person start breathing again. This treatment gets more air into the lungs than do other ways. The first step is to turn the victim's head to the side. Clean out the mouth. Take out anything that can keep air from going in. Put one hand on the forehead and the other hand under the neck. Tip the head way back, so

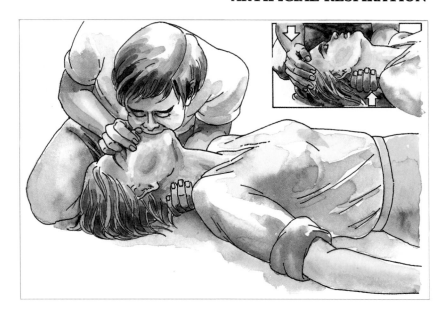

that the tongue won't block the air passage. Pinch the nose shut. Take a deep breath, open your mouth wide, and put it over the victim's mouth. Make a tight seal. Blow to fill up the lungs. Blow hard, as if you are blowing up a balloon. Watch the chest rise. Then turn your head aside and listen for air to come out. Watch the chest fall. Do these two steps over and over, once every five seconds. Keep doing this, at your normal breathing pace, listening until the victim begins breathing normally.

If you have to help a baby to start breathing again, tip the head back gently—not so far as for an adult. A baby's face is small, so you may not be able to make a seal over the mouth alone or nose alone. Put your mouth over the baby's mouth and nose. Blow gently, with small puffs of air. Blow more often—once every three seconds. Say, "Blow-listen-breathe," to a count of three.

Don't give up if the victim doesn't start breathing straightaway. You may have to try for a long time. Keep on until a doctor arrives.

A new and improved method of artificial respiration called *cardiopulmonary resuscitation* (CPR) can be learned from the Red Cross.

ALSO READ: FIRST AID, LIFESAVING.

▲ *Mouth-to-mouth breathing can save the life of a person who has stopped breathing. Learn how to perform this technique properly.*

▲ *An art museum is a place where people can see and enjoy fine works of art.*

ART MUSEUMS AND GALLERIES

Art museums are buildings in which art objects of many kinds are kept for people to see and enjoy. There is probably a museum in a city near you. Most art museums are in big cities, because it takes the support of many people to build up an art museum collection. It also takes a lot of money. The largest one in the United States is the Metropolitan Museum of Art in New York City.

An art museum often has armor, Egyptian mummies, old furniture, and other art objects as well as paintings. An art *gallery* usually specializes in paintings or sculpture. In many cities there are little galleries which operate as businesses to sell paintings. The gallery owner shares the price of each painting sold with the artist. Other galleries are run by artists themselves. The most famous little galleries are in the center of New York City. Galleries both display and sell art objects, but museums only display them.

When you go to an art museum, you may not see the busy staff who keep the museum going. The chief is called the *director*. Several *curators* work under the director. Each curator works with one kind of art. For example, one may be a curator of American paintings. There are also *conservators*, who clean and repair paintings, sculpture, and other delicate art objects. In the *education department* are art historians, who give talks to museum visitors and write about the collection.

▼ *One of the jobs of an art museum is to clean and repair old or damaged paintings. This restoration work is done by experts called conservators.*

■ LEARN BY DOING

When you visit an art museum, look at whatever *you* want to see. You don't have to see every picture. Think of your museum visit as a birthday party where you don't know every guest. You can't get to know them all, so you should look for someone you think you would like. At the museum, look for an art object you like. If you like paintings, do you want to see portraits of boys and girls from long ago? Or do you like big, splashy modern paintings? Perhaps you would like the armor collection best. Remember, you visit a museum to *look*. Let a picture or statue "speak" to you. If you have a question, ask a guide. When you get home, if you have the name of artists whose works you liked, you can read about them— perhaps in this encyclopedia. ■

ALSO READ: ART, ART HISTORY, LOUVRE.

ASIA

Asia is the largest continent. It is larger than North and South America combined and covers almost one-third of the world's land area. More than half of all the people in the world live in Asia, which also has the world's highest mountains, broadest plateaus, and largest plains.

Asia stretches 6,900 miles (11,100 km) from western Turkey northeastward to northern Siberia. In a north-south direction, the continent extends from far above the Arctic Circle to below the equator—a total distance of 5,300 miles (8,500 km). The major countries of Asia are India, China, and Japan. The Siberian part of the Soviet Union also lies in Asia. The Arabian peninsula and the Middle East are on the western fringe of Asia. (See the articles on ARABIA and the MIDDLE EAST.)

Land and Climate The borders of India, Afghanistan, the Soviet Union, and China all meet at the Pamir knot, a high place in central Asia called "the roof of the world." From this knot of cold, high, rocky land, huge mountain ranges stretch out in many directions like crooked roots of a tree. The Sulaiman and Hindu Kush mountains run hundreds of miles from the Pamirs into Southwest Asia. The Tien Shan and the Kunlun mountains extend northeast and east into China, Mongolia, and Tibet for more than 1,000 miles (1,600 km).

The mightiest mountains of all, the Karakorams and the Himalayas, branch southeast from the Pamirs and cut off the Indian subcontinent from China. Eighty-eight of the ninety highest peaks in the world are found in these two mountain ranges. Tallest of all is Mount Everest in the Himalayas. It is 29,028 feet (8, 848 m) high.

In these mountains rise many of the great rivers of Asia. On the Indian subcontinent side, the Indus, the Brahmaputra, and the Ganges begin their long routes to the Indian Ocean. North of the Himalayas in the plateau of Tibet, the Mekong River flows southward to Southeast Asia. The Yangtze and Yellow rivers flow eastward through China.

Almost every kind of climate and weather can be found somewhere in Asia. Cherrapunji, India, has more than 450 inches (11,430 mm) of rainfall a year. In contrast, less than 2 inches (58 mm) of rain fall each year in the Gobi Desert of China and Mongolia. Temperatures often go up to 120°F (49°C) in northern India during May before the rainy season. But Oymyakon, in northern Siberia, had one winter day when the temperature dropped to minus 108°F (−78°C).

Northern China and the northernmost island of Japan have weather like that of the United States' Midwest, with hot summers and cold winters. Southern Japan, southeastern China, and northern India have a subtropical climate much like that of

▲ *Farmland in Pakistan. The fields are irrigated (watered) by ditches.*

Florida. Winter is dry in India, but in Japan and eastern China rain falls in all four seasons.

Large deserts spread over much of central and southwestern Asia. The mountains surrounding these regions cut off moist air from the sea.

The climate of the Indian subcontinent, Southeast Asia, and China is controlled by powerful winds called *monsoons*. These winds change their direction with the seasons. During the summer, the monsoons blow from the southeast, off the Indian Ocean or along Asia's Pacific coast. They bring drenching rain to India and her neighbors. Sheets of water attack the land. Too much rain causes serious flooding. Crops are destroyed. During the winter, the monsoons blow from the northeast, off the land, creating a cool, dry season. Dust storms are frequent in parts of China. Too little rain destroys crops, too. The lives of hundreds of millions of people are affected by the summer or winter monsoons. Farming is usually done before and after the rainy season.

Animals Large and Small Thousands of kinds of animals live in Asia, from the mouselike gerbils of the dry, hot deserts to the 10-foot (3-m) Komodo dragon-lizards of rainy Indonesia. Many animals are native

ASIA

Total Population
3,100,000,000.

Highest Point
Mount Everest between Tibet (China) and Nepal 29,028 feet (8,848 m).

Lowest Point
Dead Sea between Israel and Jordan, 1,320 feet (402 m) below sea level.

Longest River
Yangtze River 3,716 miles (5,980 km) long.

Largest Lake
Caspian Sea 153,000 square miles (396,270 sq. km).

Largest City
Tokyo 11,800,000 people.

ARCTIC OCEAN

Yenisey

Lena

URAL MOUNTAINS

Ob

USSR

•Omsk •Novosibirsk

L. Baikal

•Irkutsk

Am

Black Sea

•Izmir ■Ankara

TURKEY

CYPRUS
Nicosia■
LEBANON
Beirut■
Jerusalem•
ISRAEL
JORDAN
•Aleppo
SYRIA
■Damascus
■Amman
IRAQ
Baghdad■
Euphrates
Tigris
Basra•
•Abadan
■Kuwait
KUWAIT

CAUCASUS

Aral Sea

Syr Darya

Caspian Sea

Amu Darya

•Tehran

•Isfahan

IRAN

AFGHANISTAN

•Kabul ■

L. Balkhash

TIEN SHAN

Ulan Bator■

MONGOLIA

Hwang Ho Peki

Gobi Desert T

•Lanchow

•Sian

CHINA

•Islamabad
Lahore•Kashmir

Tibet

HIMALAYAS

•Lhasa

Chengtu•

Yangtze-Kiang

•Chungking

•Medina

•Riyadh■

BAHRAIN
QATAR
■Doha

UAE

Jeddah• •Mecca

Arabian Desert

Red Sea

SAUDI
ARABIA

OMAN

■Muscat

San'a■
YEMEN
SOUTH YEMEN

■Aden

PAKISTAN

Indus

Karachi•

•Hyderabad

•Ahmadabad

•Bombay

Kunming•

Si-Kia

PAKISTAN

New Delhi■ •Delhi

NEPAL
Katmandu
Mt
•Everest▲
Kanpur• •Lucknow
•Varanasi

Thimphu
■
BHUTAN

Brahmaputra

BURMA

•Mandalay

Hanoi■

LAOS

Vientiane■

VIETNAM

Mekong

INDIA

Ganges

Calcutta•

BANGLADESH

■Dacca

Irrawaddy

Salween

Rangoon•

•Nagpur

Godavari

•Hyderabad

Bangalore• •Madras

SRI
LANKA

Colombo■

THAILAND

Bangkok•

KAMPUCHEA

Phnom Penh■

Saigon
(Ho Chi Min

MALDIVE IS

•Malé

ASIA

0   400   800   1200 miles

0   400   800 1200 1600 kilometers

■ Capital Cities

INDIAN   OCEAN

Penang•

MALAYSIA

•Kuala Lumpur

■SINGAPORE

Sumatra

I

•Djakart

ASIAN NATIONS

Country	Area in Square Miles	Area in Square Kilometers	Capital	Population
Afghanistan	250,018	647,497	Kabul	16,590,000
Bangladesh	55,602	143,998	Dacca	112,760,000
Bhutan	18,148	47,000	Thimphu	1,530,000
Brunei	2,226	5,765	Bandar Seri Begawan	267,000
Burma (Myanmar)	261,237	676,552	Rangoon	39,900,000
China	3,705,676	9,596,961	Beijing (Peking)	1,070,000,000
Hong Kong	403	1,045	Victoria	5,700,000
India	1,269,437	3,287,590	New Delhi	833,000,000
Indonesia	782,719	2,027,087	Jakarta	188,000,000
Japan	143,761	372,313	Tokyo	123,000,000
Kampuchea	69,903	181,035	Phnom Penh	6,850,000
North Korea	46,543	120,538	Pyongyang	22,000,000
South Korea	38,028	98,484	Seoul	45,240,000
Laos	91,436	236,800	Vientiane	3,900,000
Macao	6	16	Macao City	430,000
Malaysia	127,326	329,749	Kuala Lumpur	16,900,000
Maldive Islands	115	298	Malé	200,000
Mongolia	604,294	1,565,000	Ulan Bator	2,000,000
Nepal	54,366	140,797	Katmandu	18,700,000
Pakistan	310,427	803,943	Islamabad	110,300,000
Philippines	115,839	300,000	Manila	62,000,000
Singapore	224	581	Singapore	2,700,000
Sri Lanka	25,334	65,610	Colombo	17,500,000
Taiwan (Formosa)	13,885	35,961	Taipei	20,300,000
Thailand	198,471	514,000	Bangkok	55,000,000
Vietnam	127,251	329,556	Hanoi	66,700,000

(*Note*—For information on the U.S.S.R. (Russia), see the table with the article on EUROPE.
For information on southwestern Asian nations, see the tables with the articles on ARABIA and MIDDLE EAST.)

P A C I F I C   O C E A N

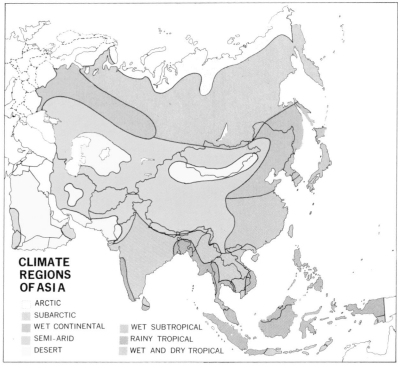

CLIMATE REGIONS OF ASIA

- ARCTIC
- SUBARCTIC
- WET CONTINENTAL
- SEMI-ARID
- DESERT
- WET SUBTROPICAL
- RAINY TROPICAL
- WET AND DRY TROPICAL

only to Asia. Some of these are the Lake Baikal seal of the Soviet Union; the snow leopard, found in the U.S.S.R. and China; the Siberian tiger; the orangutan of Borneo and Sumatra; and the giant panda of China, a black and white bearlike animal.

Tigers, apes, monkeys, elephants, and rhinoceroses live in Southeast Asia. In dry Southwest Asia gazelles live in the hills. The domesticated camel was once the most important means of transportation in many desert areas of Asia.

Asia is home to a wide range of birds, from the subarctic Siberian murre to the lammergeier, a huge Indian vulture, to the beautiful peacock and lyrebird of Indonesia. Snakes, many poisonous, are plentiful in parts of Asia. Crocodiles live in southern Asia's rivers and lakes, as do many fish.

The wet, tropical regions of Asia have many kinds of insects, some of which carry serious disease. Mosquitoes, for example, thrive in southern Asia, spreading malaria, although DDT (a powerful insecticide) has helped control this dread disease.

People The peoples of Asia are often separated from each other by scorching deserts, dense jungles, and rugged mountain ranges. Transportation overland is difficult in some places, even today. It is not surprising that thousands of years ago many groups of people never knew they had neighbors. Separated from each other, Asian peoples developed different religions, languages, styles of art, forms of government, and cultures, or ways of life.

Many Asians are farmers who live in small villages in river valleys in many areas of the continent. They often follow the customs and habits of their ancestors, although new farming methods are changing their lives.

Millions of Asians live in cities that sprawl along the banks of rivers and harbors. Waterfronts, marketplaces, and streets are jammed with people, animals, wagons, bicycles, cars, buses, and trucks. Life is far more crowded than in Western cities. In Japan, men called "pushers" pack persons into overcrowded trains and buses. Tokyo, Japan, is the most populous Asian city, with more than 11 million persons. Other Asian cities with many millions include Shanghai, Peking (Beijing), and Hong Kong in China; Calcutta and Bombay in India; and Seoul in South Korea. One Asian out of three lives in a city.

Asia has many types of people. There are three main groups, each of which is concentrated in its own part of the continent. *Caucasoids* include the Iranians, Indians, Afghans, Pakistanis, and Arabs. These peoples live in western Asia and the Indian subcontinent. *Mongoloids*, including the Chinese, Koreans, and Japanese, live in the Far East. Small groups of *Negroids* live in the Philippine Islands and the Malay Peninsula.

LANGUAGES. Languages vary so much in Asia that in some parts people in one village speak differently from people in a neighboring village a few miles away. Most Indians speak

Hindi, the official language of India, but English is widely used for business and official communications. Fourteen major languages and hundreds of dialects are spoken in India. The Chinese, Tibetan, Burmese, and Thai languages are related to each other, but a speaker of one of these languages will not understand the others. Nearly four times as many people speak them as live in the U.S. The Altaic language family includes Turkish, Mongol, and Manchu. Japanese and Korean may be eastern extensions of the Altaic family. People of Southeast Asia also use many different tongues of the Malayo-Polynesian language family. These include Malay, Javanese, Tagalog, and Balinese.

RELIGION. In this vast continent, with so many peoples and ways of living, there are several religions. All of the world's major religions began in Asia. Hinduism and Buddhism started in India, Judaism and Christianity in the Middle East, Islam in Arabia, Confucianism and Taoism in China, and Shintoism in Japan. These religions have hundreds of millions of followers, and all of them have helped shape the history of the world.

Natural Resources Asia is both a rich and a poor land. Its total farm production is the world's highest, but millions of Asians sometimes go hungry. Millions of tons of rice—the most important Asian crop—are grown each year. Rice plants are usually set into flooded fields, called *paddies*. Wheat is grown instead of rice in parts of China, Siberia, and the Indian subcontinent, where less rain falls. Poor Asian peasants often work on huge plantations in Southeast Asia, growing enormous crops of rubber, tea, coffee, sugar, and spices. Most of these crops are exported to other continents.

Huge timber forests cover part of Siberia. Exotic woods, such as teak and sandalwood, are shipped all over the world from the tropical forests of Southeast Asia. In some areas, cutting down the forests has caused problems of land erosion.

Fish is a major food of many Asians. Commerical fishing is very important and highly developed in some Asian countries. The annual fish catch of Japan is the greatest in the world. Asia is rich in many mineral resources. One-half of all the known oil reserves in the world are in Southwest Asia, mainly in the countries around the Persian Gulf. Borneo and Indonesia in Southeast Asia also have valuable oil fields. Many other minerals, such as bauxite, chromium, coal, copper, iron, manganese, and tin, are found in large quantities in Asia.

Asia had no important industry until the 1900's. But now Japan is the third major industrial power in the world, after the United States and the Soviet Union. India and China are also building many new factories that produce steel, farm equipment, and fertilizer. Other countries, such as the

▲ *A woman from Burma and a man from Pakistan. The Burmese are related to the Mongoloid peoples of China in eastern Asia. The Pakistanis are a mixture of peoples from western Asia. The main religion in Burma is Buddhism. In Pakistan, it is Islam. Burmese is the chief language of Burma. In Pakistan, it is Urdu.*

◄ *A Muslim mosque. Every day in Islamic countries of Asia the faithful are summoned to prayer.*

▲ *Tea is an important crop in South Asia, including India and Sri Lanka. The leaves are picked by hand.*

▼ *Flooded ricefields in the Philippines, in Southeast Asia. Every inch of farmland is put to use, by cutting out terraces from hillsides.*

Republic of Korea, are now producing many goods, including cars, textiles, and electronics parts. Because wages are low, Asian-made goods are often less expensive than those made elsewhere in the world.

Ancient and Modern Asia has probably been home to humans for at least 500,000 years. Scientists have found traces of early people in Asia. A skull, called *Peking Man*, is one of the oldest fossils that hints at human history. The skull was found near Peking, China, in 1929. The oldest cities in the world were built in Asia more than 4,000 years ago. One such ancient civilization was in the Indus River Valley of present-day Pakistan. Other ancient civilizations appeared about the same time in other parts of the continent. China had perhaps the greatest civilization of all.

Many of these great civilizations were ravaged in the 13th century by hordes of Mongols, tribes who came from central Asia. The Mongol Empire once extended all the way from China to the **Black Sea**. Turkish armies took over after the Mongols in some areas.

The riches of Asia—silks, spices, and jewels—attracted traders and explorers from Europe. Starting in the 1500's, many European countries claimed parts of Asia as colonies. China and **Japan** feared Europe and closed their ports to most foreigners. In the 19th century, Western nations negotiated treaties that opened Asian ports to foreign trade.

Hundreds of millions of Asians gained freedom from Western colonial rule after World War II. They include Indians, Pakistanis, Burmese, Filipinos, Indonesians, Malaysians, and Indochinese. Hong Kong is a British colony until it is returned to China in 1997; Macao remains a Portuguese overseas province.

The People's Republic of China has a Communist government. This government adopted a freer and more Western-looking policy in the 1980's. The most economically advanced country in Asia, Japan, is a constitu-

▼ *Asia is a continent of contrasts. Herdsmen with their flocks may be seen alongside industrial plants.*

tional monarchy. India is the world's largest nation with a democratic form of government. Like almost everything else, political forms are varied in this largest and most populous of continents.

For further information on:
Arts, *see* ART HISTORY, FOLK ART, MUSICAL INSTRUMENTS, ORIENTAL ART, PAGODA, TAJ MAHAL.
History, *see* ANCIENT CIVILIZATIONS; CHENG HO; CHIANG KAI-SHEK; CHOU EN-LAI; GANDHI, INDIRA; GANDHI, MAHATMA; GENGHIS KHAN; MAO TSETUNG; NEHRU, JAWAHARLAL; POLO, MARCO; SUN YAT-SEN; TENG HSIAO P'ING.
Language, *see* ARABIC, CHINESE, LANGUAGES, RUSSIAN.
Human Life, *see* CIVILIZATION, HUMAN BEING.
Physical Features, *see* ARAL SEA, ARCTIC LIFE, BLACK SEA, CAUCASUS MOUNTAINS, DESERT, GANGES RIVER, GOBI DESERT, HIMALAYA MOUNTAINS, MIDDLE EAST, PEKING, SHANGHAI, SOUTHEAST ASIA.
Also read the article on each country shown in the table.

ASS see DONKEY.

ASSASSINATION When a person murders a president or king or some other important person, the crime is often called an assassination. The murderer is called an *assassin.*

These words came from a group of Muslims who lived more than 900 years ago in Syria and Persia. Before being sent to kill an enemy, a man was always given the drug *hashish* to make him crazy and reckless. From the Arabic name for these men, *hashshashin,* comes the English word "assassin."

An assassin may give several reasons for his act. He or she may kill for revenge—to punish the victim for some harm (real or imagined) done to

◀ *This three-tiered Japanese pavilion is a fine example of the gentle beauty of Asian architecture.*

▲ *Asia's most powerful industrial nation is Japan. Tokyo, Japan's capital, is a busy and crowded city.*

the assassin. An assassin may kill a government leader, either because he thinks the leader is evil or because he wishes to take over control of the government himself. An assassin may even be paid to kill. Whatever the reason, all assassins are *fanatics* who think that whatever they do must be right.

Assassins have killed four United States Presidents—Abraham Lincoln, James Garfield, William McKinley, and John F. Kennedy. Others failed to assassinate Presidents Andrew Jackson, Theodore Roosevelt, Franklin D. Roosevelt, Harry Truman, Gerald R. Ford, and Ronald Reagan.

ALSO READ: CAESAR, JULIUS; GANDHI, MAHATMA; GANDHI, INDIRA; GARFIELD, JAMES A.; KENNEDY, JOHN F.; KING, MARTIN LUTHER, JR.; LINCOLN, ABRAHAM; MALCOLM X; MCKINLEY, WILLIAM; TERRORISM.

When John F. Kennedy was assassinated in 1963, a strange tradition continued. Every American president since William H. Harrison who was elected in a year ending in "0" has died while still in office. Harrison was elected in 1840, Abraham Lincoln in 1860, James A. Garfield in 1880, William McKinley in 1900, Warren G. Harding in 1920, Franklin D. Roosevelt in 1940, and John F. Kennedy in 1960.

245

ASSYRIA

▶ *The Assyrians ruled the land between the headwaters of the river Tigris and Euphrates. To the south were the rich civilizations of Babylonia and Sumer. The Assyrian empire stretched as far west as Egypt.*

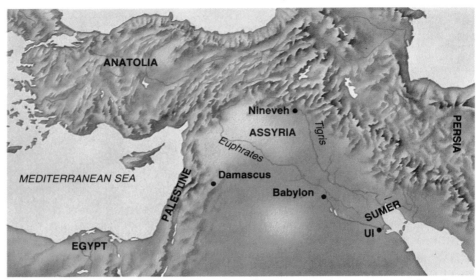

Assyrian kings collected large libraries of clay tablets with cuneiform writing. King Ashurbanipal's large library, discovered in the 1800's, had tablets on medicine, history, religion, literature, and many other subjects.

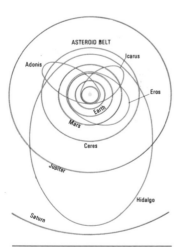

▲ *Most of the asteroids move around the sun in a wide belt between the orbits of the planets Mars and Jupiter. The largest, Ceres, is of this type. But some others, as shown in this diagram, have eccentric orbits that take them beyond the belt.*

ASSYRIA Assyria was an ancient kingdom on the upper Tigris River in the country now known as Iraq. Assyrians were great warriors. They invented iron weapons and, by superb organization, they conquered Babylonia to the south, Syria and Israel to the west, and northern Egypt in the 800's and 700's B.C. (See the map with the article on ANCIENT CIVILIZATIONS.) The Assyrian Empire lasted only until 612 B.C., when Babylonia and Media conquered Assyria.

Assyria's main god was Assur, the god of war. Assyria's religion, arts, and customs were mostly borrowed from the Babylonians. Military power was all-important. Merchants' caravans that crossed the Tigris River were charged tolls to pay for the Assyrian armies. King Sennacherib built the Assyrian capital Nineveh about 700 B.C. He made it a magnificent armed camp. The laws of Assyria were harsh. As punishment, entire tribes were forcibly moved to another part of the empire.

Many pieces of Assyrian art from the empire period have been found. Most of their sculpture was done in *relief*, that is, shallow carving on stone. Figures of kings and gods were carved on the walls of buildings. Whole walls were used to show scenes of the Assyrian conquest. Some scenes were cruel. Among the most famous sculptures are the large Winged Bulls, which stood before the king's palace to impress visitors.

ALSO READ: ANCIENT CIVILIZATIONS, BABYLONIA, IRAQ, MESOPOTAMIA, SYRIA, TIGRIS-EUPHRATES RIVER.

ASTEROID The thousands of chunks of metal and rock, which circle the sun between the orbits of the planets Mars and Jupiter, are called asteroids or minor planets.

Only a few of them are large enough to be seen without a powerful telescope. The largest, Ceres, is only 620 miles (998 km) in diameter. Earth's moon has a diameter 3½ times that size.

Asteroids were discovered almost by accident. Eighteenth-century astronomers believed there was a planet in an orbit, or path, between Mars and Jupiter. By 1800, a great search was underway to locate the new planet. On January 1, 1801, an Italian astronomer, Giuseppe Piazzi, spotted a small dot of light that he had never seen before. He named it Ceres. It was too small to be the missing planet, but astronomers soon decided that Ceres was in orbit where the planet should be.

The mystery was solved when astronomers discovered more asteroids orbiting near Ceres. Instead of one large planet, over 3,000 tiny ones have been found. Many are only one or two miles (2–3 km) across. A few asteroids pass closer to the sun than the inner planet Mercury, while another, Chiron, is farther away than Saturn.

Some of the asteroids may be fragments of two or more small planets that collided and broke up. Others may be tiny embryonic planets that never grew larger. But even if all the asteroids were collected together, they would make a body much smaller than the moon.

ALSO READ: SOLAR SYSTEM.

Find your birthday according to the calender	What is your birth sign according to the astrological calendar?	
Your Birthday	**Sign of the Zodiac**	
January 21— February 19	Aquarius, the Water Bearer	♒
February 20—March 20	Pisces, the Fish	♓
March 21—April 20	Aries, the Ram	♈
April 21—May 22	Taurus, the Bull	♉
May 23—June 21	Gemini, the Twins	♊
June 22—July 22	Cancer, the Crab	♋
July 23—August 22	Leo, the Lion	♌
August 23—September 22	Virgo, the Virgin	♍
September 23—October 22	Libra, the Scales	♎
October 23—November 21	Scorpio, the Scorpion	♏
November 22—December 22	Sagittarius, the Archer	♐
December 23—January 20	Capricorn, the Sea Goat	♑

ASTROLOGY Astrology is the belief that the movements of the planets, stars, moon, and sun affect people's lives. Astrologers were among the first people to measure the movements of the heavenly bodies. They helped start the science of astronomy.

Ancient people often used astrology in their religion. Chaldeans and Babylonians believed that the stars caused events and actions to happen here on Earth. The priests said that each person's life depended on the positions of the planets when the person was born. A person's future was decided at the moment of his or her birth. The priests claimed they could tell their kings the future. If the planets were in "bad" positions, the country would have trouble. Plans were made for weddings and wars only after checking first with astrologers.

Astrology is based on the *zodiac*, the imaginary circle in the sky in which the sun, moon, and planets move. Also in this circle are 12 constellations, or groups of stars that look like different shapes. Each shape is a *sign* of the zodiac, or a month in the astrologer's calendar.

After learning a person's birth date, an astrologer makes a *horoscope*. This is a map of the sun and planets within the constellations on the birth date. From a horoscope, an astrologer tries to tell what will presently happen to a person. Astrologers believe that people born under each sign of the zodiac have special character traits.

Astrology is still practiced today. Some people will not make a major decision without a prediction from an astrologer. Many others think astrology is merely fun or nonsense.

■ LEARN BY DOING

Find your own sign of the zodiac on the table. Each day for a week, read the section in your newspaper possibly called "Star Gazing" or "Your Horoscope." Did anything that was predicted actually come true for you? ■

ALSO READ: ASTRONOMY, CONSTELLATION, MYTHOLOGY.

◄ *This picture shows all the signs of the zodiac. Can you find your birthday sign?*

▲ *Yuri Gagarin of the Soviet Union, first astronaut to orbit the Earth in 1961. The first woman in space was Soviet cosmonaut Valentina Tereshkova.*

▼ *Blast-off of the first U.S. space shuttle,* Columbia, *in 1981. The shuttle was the world's first reusable spacecraft.*

▶ *Buzz Aldrin, Apollo 11 astronaut, on the moon. You can see the photographer, Neil Armstrong, reflected in the visor of Aldrin's space helmet.*

ASTRONAUT Alan B. Shepard, Jr., in his *Freedom 7* spacecraft, was launched into space from Cape Canaveral, Florida, by a Redstone rocket on May 5, 1961. Shepard was the first American in space. He was also one of America's first seven astronauts. The others were Virgil I. Grissom, Donald K. Slayton, John H. Glenn, Jr., Malcolm S. Carpenter, Walter M. Schirra, and Leroy G. Cooper, Jr. "Astronaut" comes from the Greek words *astron* ("star") and *nautes* ("sailor"). In the Soviet Union, astronauts are called *cosmonauts*.

To pilot a spaceship, a person must pass many tests. Most astronauts must be jet pilots, and all astronauts must be very healthy. They cannot be too fat or too skinny, too tall or too short. They must be trained in a wide variety of complex subjects.

Astronauts are trained by the National Aeronautics and Space Administration (NASA), in Houston, Texas. Those who cannot fly spend a year learning to fly jets. They begin general training when they can fly. They learn about mechanics, guidance and

control, communication, navigation, astronomy, and geology. Geology is one of the most important subjects they study. They take field trips to Iceland, Hawaii, Nevada, and Alaska to learn about rock formations and how to use certain tools and maps.

Each astronaut is assigned to a crew. He or she trains for one special job to be done during a space flight. The trainee astronauts must fly jet trainers in practice sessions at least three times a week. They may spend thousands of hours "flying" in *simulators*. Simulators are special training machines and equipment that look exactly like real spacecraft equipment. In the simulators, astronauts learn to pilot the spacecraft, until they can do everything automatically. They must learn how every piece of equipment works, how to navigate (control the course of the spacecraft), how to handle emergencies, and how it feels to be weightless. In case of a forced landing, astronauts must also have jungle and desert survival training. They also learn to perform experiments, take photographs, and walk in space.

But the United States space program also needs to send expert specialists into space. The first scientist-astronaut was the geologist Harrison Schmitt, who went to the moon in 1972. Since then, the Space Shuttle, which can carry up to five passengers and two crew members, has taken non-astronaut civilians into orbit around Earth.

ALSO READ: ALDRIN, EDWIN; ARMSTRONG, NEIL; COLLINS, MICHAEL; GAGARIN, YURI; GLENN, JOHN; SHEPARD, ALAN B.; SPACE TRAVEL.

ASTRONOMY People have always looked up at the sky and asked questions about what they saw. What makes the sun shine? What makes it warm? What are the stars, the moon, the planets? Astronomers are the people who try to answer these questions. Astronomy is the study of the *heavenly bodies*, all the objects in the sky. It is the oldest science.

One task of astronomy is to keep track of all the heavenly bodies. What time will the sun rise? What time will it set? When will winter begin? When will it be warm enough to plant crops? These questions were very important to the first astronomers. They are still important to farmers, sailors, pilots, astronauts, and many other people.

Ancient astronomers studied the objects in the sky for a very long time. They finally began to notice patterns—events that happened again and again. One important pattern they saw was the *phases of the moon*. If you look at the moon every night for a month, you will see the changes, or phases, it goes through. At the beginning of the pattern, the moon does not shine. The next night, it looks like a very thin piece of a circle. We call both of these "shapes" the *new moon*. Each night for a week, the curved, shiny piece grows bigger. At the end of the week, a half circle glows in the sky. Two weeks after the new moon, we see the *full moon*, a bright, shiny circle. Then, every night for two weeks, less and less of the circle shines. Finally, one night the moon "disappears" again. We are back to the start of the pattern, the new moon. Astronomers invented the first calendar using this pattern. Early calendars were not as accurate as the calendars of today. But they helped farmers and sailors, just as today's calendars help people.

■ LEARN BY DOING

You can "discover" the moon, just as these ancient astronomers did. Begin with a full moon. What time does it rise? Keep a daily time chart by *your* clock. Does your time agree with the time shown in your newspaper? Draw the moon. You can see details with a telescope or binoculars, but remember that ancient astronomers did not have these tools.

Keep a daily record from one full moon to the next. How many days does this take?

What if clouds hide the moon on a few nights—or even just one? Can you guess how it looked on that night? Can you guess when it rose? Record that you did not see the moon on those nights. Check your guesses by watching the next cycle of the moon. You may have to make several observations to see the moon in all its phases.

As the moon circles the Earth, it "hides" several stars—Aldebaran, Regulus, Spica, Antares, and the Pleiades. Try to watch one of these *occultations* (hidings). How long does it last? What might an ancient observer have thought about this? ■

Astronomers in the ancient world could measure many things that happened in the sky. But they could not explain why these things happened. The second main task of astronomy is to explain the *causes* of events in the sky. The ancient Chinese built a big observatory some 4,600 years ago. They could predict *when* eclipses would occur, but they did not know how to explain what happened. The darkness scared them. People believed an eclipse happened because a dragon tried to swallow the sun. People in many different countries made up *myths*, or imaginary stories, to explain events in the sky they could not understand. Ancient Greek astronomers made the most progress in explaining how some things happen in the sky.

Greek Astronomy The most difficult problem was to explain how and why the heavenly bodies seem to circle the Earth. Pythagoras, in the 500's B.C., and then Aristarchus, three centuries later, taught that the planets revolved around the sun. But not many people believed them. Plato

▲ *A Mesopotamian "star map." Three thousand years old, this stone tablet shows the constellation Scorpio as well as the moon and the planet Venus.*

▲ *Medieval astronomers at work in an observatory at Istanbul, in Turkey.*

▲ *Isaac Newton built the first reflector telescope in 1668.*

▲ *One of the world's largest optical telescopes is the Mayall reflector at Kitt Peak, Arizona. Its mirror is 158 inches (4 m) across. The world's largest telescope is now in the Soviet Union. It has a mirror 236.2 inches (6 m) in diameter.*

▶ *The Hale Telescope on Palomar Mountain, near Pasadena, California, was the world's largest until 1976. Its main mirror is 200 inches (5 m) across.*

and Aristotle, two important philosophers and astronomers, taught that Earth is the center of the universe. They thought the sun, moon, stars, and planets were attached to giant spheres rotating around the Earth. This seemed easier to believe. Claudius Ptolemy, a Greek who lived in Egypt around A.D. 100 to 170, believed what Aristotle and Plato taught. He wrote 13 books that "proved" the Earth is the center of the universe. For centuries many people believed he was right.

Nicolaus Copernicus, a Polish astronomer of the 1500's, claimed that all the planets revolved around the sun. Again, people said he was wrong. But a few astronomers listened to him and made great discoveries. A Danish astronomer, Tycho Brahe, measured the movements of all the heavenly bodies he could see in the late 1500's. He made careful records. Johannes Kepler, a German scientist, used Brahe's measurements to show that Earth and all other planets *orbit* (circle) the sun. Galileo, an Italian, described this fact after he started using a telescope.

Modern Astronomy The telescope was the tool that finally helped astronomers understand the movements of the heavenly bodies. Even a small telescope made a great difference. Galileo was the first astronomer to use one. It was not very powerful when compared to today's telescopes. But using this tool, he was able to see things that no one had ever seen before. In 1610, he discovered four moons of Jupiter. (Jupiter really has at least 17 moons, but the others are so small Galileo could not see them with his weak telescope.)

When he saw these four moons orbiting around Jupiter, Galileo knew that Aristotle was wrong to say that everything in the universe revolves around the Earth. He also discovered that the planet Venus must revolve around the sun, because it shows phases, like the phases of the moon, as we see different parts of it lit up by the sun.

Over 350 years have passed since Galileo's discovery. Scientists have been making bigger and bigger telescopes since Galileo first used one. Astronomers now have other impor-

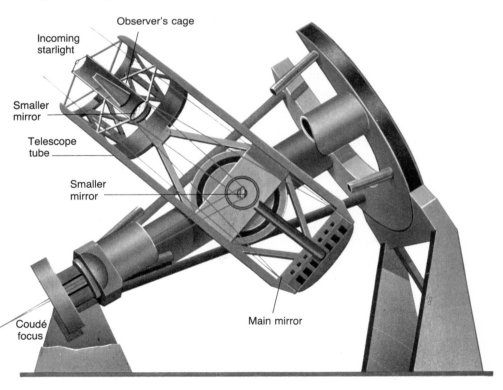

tant tools, too. A camera is as important as a telescope to today's astronomer. Astronomers often use them together. They take special photographs called *time exposures*. To make these photographs the light of stars is allowed to shine on film for hours, instead of just part of a second. These photographs reveal stars whose light is too faint to see, even with a telescope. Astronomers often discover comets and asteroids "by accident" on time exposures. A comet or asteroid shows up on film as a line of light. Stars look like dots.

Another important tool is the *spectrograph*. It "examines" and separates a ray of light into the different colors in it. When light from a star shines through a spectrograph, an expert looks to see how much of each color is in the light. He can tell what a star is made of from looking at the different colors in the spectrum.

Many objects in the universe send out radio waves. These were first detected, accidentally, in 1932, and since that time radio astronomers have made many important discoveries. For example, the space between stars in the galaxy contains very fine, scattered dust, which blocks out light from other objects beyond—but radio waves sent out by these objects can pass through the dust and be received by radio telescopes. Some of the most distant galaxies in the universe send out radio waves very strongly. Radio telescopes usually have a big curved metal "dish" to focus the radio waves.

Today's astronomers have brand-new tools—radio astronomy, X-ray astronomy, and space travel. Man-made orbiting satellites and rockets fly above Earth's atmosphere, where they take clearer photographs of the sun and planets than were ever taken before. Astronauts have walked on the moon; space probes have flown past other planets. Probes have landed on Mercury, Venus, and Mars and flown by the outer planets, such as Jupiter and Uranus.

The Universe No one knew the size of the universe in ancient times. Ptolemy knew that stars are farther away from Earth than the planets are. But, if you could talk to Ptolemy, and tell him how far away the stars really are, or how far even the planets are he would probably not believe you. They are so distant that astronomers have had to invent new units of measurement.

If you said that New York and San Francisco are about 190,080,000 inches (482,803,200 cm) apart, you would be right. But most people would be confused, because this number is too large to understand easily. This is one reason people use *miles* or *kilometers* as a unit of measure. People usually say the two cities are about 3,000 miles (4,830 km) apart. Astronomers have the same problem except more so. Distances in space are so long that even miles or kilometers do not tell how far away the objects in space are. So astronomers use other measuring units. To measure distances inside the *solar system*—the sun and its nine planets—astronomers use the *astronomical unit* (a.u.). One a.u. is the mean distance from Earth to the sun, about 93 million miles (150 million km). Astronomers say Pluto is about 39 a.u. from the sun. This is easier than saying 3,670,000,000 miles.

The first accurate measure of the distance to the stars was made in 1838. It was discovered that even the nearest star is a quarter of a million times as far away as the sun. This means that if an orange in New York represents the sun in size, then another orange representing its neighbor would have to be placed in Las Vegas. Astronomical units are much too small for these huge spaces, so astronomers measure the distances between the stars in *light years*, which is a short way of saying, the distance that light travels in a year. Light travels about 186,000 miles (300,000 km) in a second. In a year, that adds

▲ *Radio telescopes have dish antennas to pick up long-wave electromagnetic radiation from distant star clusters.*

▼ *The planet Saturn is the second largest in the sun's planet system. Its rings are more prominent than the similar rings around Jupiter and Uranus.*

up to 5,870,000,000,000 miles (9,461,000,000,000 km). Light from the stars travels a long time to reach the Earth. The nearest star to Earth is Alpha Centauri. Its light takes about four years and four months to travel the distance to Earth. Even light from the sun takes about eight minutes to journey to Earth.

The sun is an average kind of star. It belongs, with about 100 billion other stars, to the Milky Way galaxy. A galaxy is a huge group of stars of all kinds. They may be much hotter or cooler than the sun, and much larger or smaller. All the stars seen in the night sky belong to our galaxy. Looking out into space, millions of other galaxies come into view as faint smudges of light. Some of these contain ten times as many stars as our own, but others may have only a hundredth as many. We should not be too ashamed of the size and importance of our galaxy.

Astronomers can now "see" at least 10 billion light years away from Earth. Shining at this huge distance, only the very powerful galaxies known as *quasars* are bright enough to be made out. All distant galaxies are being carried away from our own galaxy at thousands of miles a second, because the universe is expanding. If their speeds and distances are calcu-

▲ *U.S. Voyager spacecraft have flown far into space to study the distant planets.*

lated backward, it looks as if all the galaxies in the universe were close together between about 15 and 20 billion years ago. Most astronomers believe that this is when the *Big Bang* occurred, and that the atomic particles which form everything, from microbes to galaxies, came into existence in one amazing explosion. As astronomers develop bigger and better telescopes, they see farther and farther out into space and learn more and more about our amazing universe.

For further information on:
Astronomers, *see* BRAHE, TYCHO; COPERNICUS, NICOLAUS; EINSTEIN, ALBERT; GALILEO; HERSCHEL FAMILY; KEPLER, JOHANNES.
Astronomers at Work, *see* LIGHT, OBSERVATORY, PLANETARIUM, RADIO ASTRONOMY, SPACE RESEARCH, SPECTRUM, STATISTICS, TELESCOPE.
Beyond the Solar System, *see* CONSTELLATION, MILKY WAY, NORTH STAR, STAR, UNIVERSE.
History, *see* ASTROLOGY, CALENDAR, EARTH HISTORY.
Solar System, *see* ASTEROID, COMET, ECLIPSE, GRAVITY, METEOR, MOON, RADIATION BELT, SOLAR SYSTEM, SUN.